# *Listening* Through *Luke*

## A Former Pastor's Self Reflection Journey Through The Gospel Story of Jesus As Told By Luke

### MARK BRAGUE

**SHINE**
PRESS

Tampa, Florida

Publisher: Shine Press
4522 W. Village Dr. #1294
Tampa, Florida 34624
Shine-Press.com | Jodi@Shine-Press.com
Shine Press is an imprint of Jodi K Costa, LLC.




Scripture quotations marked (NIV) are taken from the Holy Bible, New International Version®, NIV®. Copyright © 1973, 1978, 1984, 2011 by Biblica, Inc.™ Used by permission of Zondervan. All rights reserved worldwide. www.zondervan.com. The "NIV" and "New International Version" are trademarks registered in the United States Patent and Trademark Office by Biblica, Inc.™

For speaking engagements, event invitations, bulk orders, and other author requests, please contact the publisher: Jodi@Shine-Press.com

# FIRST EDITION


ISBN: 979-8-9937924-9-1

# PRAISES FOR
## LISTENING THROUGH LUKE

*I think a lot of guys are tired of Christian content that feels like behavior modification, or religious vocabulary with no encounter behind it. Mark's writing has 'encounter' in it. It invites a man into a decision without shaming him. It basically says: you don't have to fake it, but you also can't stay neutral. Jesus is asking you personally.*

*This isn't a book about "how to be a better man" with Jesus sprinkled on top. It is about Jesus. Period. And because of that, it naturally calls the reader upward without forcing it. That's the kind of writing which actually forms people instead of just informing them.*

*It encouraged me personally as I read it. This hit me as a reminder that the core question is not "what are you doing for God" but "who is Jesus to you, right now, in your actual life." It made me want to answer Him again, not out of obligation, but out of desire.*

## Kyle Robinson
Pastor, New York Times Best Seller, Entrepreneur, EPIC Bro.

*Mark has been in ministry longer than I have been alive. (I'm not sure if he wants me to share that!) But his experience shines through in the most refreshing way. He isn't overly academic. He's real. Mark has a gift for simplifying complex life challenges and reshaping your perspective with God's truth.*

*Reading Listening Through Luke feels like sitting down for a conversation with him, who I consider to be a trusted mentor and friend. You'll find healing, hope and practical wisdom without any of the religious fluff.*

## Blake McLemore
Attorney, Entrepreneur, Epic Bro.

*So much of life feels rushed. "Get it done quickly! Are you finished yet?" But reading Mark's Listening Through Luke slowed me down. In my mind, I found myself sitting on a front porch, a glass of lemonade in my hand, talking with old friends. There was no hurry. Just time. Time to listen, to reflect and hear Mark's practical thoughtful insights about God, Jesus, and how our everyday lives fit into God's bigger story.*

*Mark has a gift for helping Luke's Gospel feel both simple and deeply meaningful. He doesn't rush past the words. He invites you to sit with them, and in doing so encounter Jesus in a way that feels real, human and unforced.*

## David Monson
Pastor, Entrepreneur, EPIC Bro.

God has certainly chiseled Mark into a man that craves sincerity. If something (or someone) whiffs of insincerity, you might find Mark heading for the exit! All that to say, in this devotional you are getting the real Mark—sincere, witty, honest, and tender. If your heart is longing for a touch from a true friend, I encourage you to read this devotional!

## Clay Jones
Ministry Student, Husband, Father of 4, Secret HS Agent, EPIC bro

This book has been such a gift to me. Mark draws beautiful revelation out of passages that have become overly familiar to many. The way he provides context creates space for reflection and deeper understanding, all within a structure and tone that make the book easy to read and digest on a daily basis.

For me, reading often feels like a chore. But after picking up this book, I genuinely look forward to starting my day in Luke. The prayers and prompts at the end of each chapter help move the truth from my head to my heart, allowing me to apply what I'm learning and grow in unexpected ways.

This is a book I will return to again and again—one that continually reminds me that Jesus came down for me, and that His kingdom is not merely a set of ideals or moral teachings, but a relationship meant to be lived out through real human experience.

Reading this has drawn me closer to Jesus and reminded me that He calls me friend. Friendship with Jesus is never urgent, but it is deeply important. It is where life truly flows from, and I'm grateful to have been reminded of the beauty and benefit of drawing near to the One who created me

## Bill Stainback
Husband, Father of 5, Airline Pilot, Veteran, EPIC Bro.

Reading through Luke with Mark is honest, unhurried, and refreshingly human, not unlike Mark himself. This is the kind of writing that doesn't try to fix you, shame you or guilt you but it invites you along. And somehow, without pressure, you find yourself wanting to delve deeper in seeking Jesus, not because you should, but because you actually want to.

## Harvey Rowland
Entrepreneur, Veteran, Proper Britt, EPIC Bro.

I highly recommend this book for anyone who desires a deeper walk with the Lord and the men in your life. Mark's ability to take you where he has been is remarkable. His commentary is so rich and real that you will want to read it daily and be eager for the next installment. It was an honor to walk with him through this.

## Paul Ziga
Husband, Father, Accounting Leader, EPIC Bro.

*This devotional on the Gospel of Luke is honestly unlike anything I've read. It slows you down and invites you to look beyond the English words on the page, drawing insight from the original Greek in a way that feels natural and meaningful, not academic.*

*Written by a lifelong friend, this book is shaped by Jewish heritage, time spent in Israel, and years of walking with God—and it shows. Luke's Gospel comes alive as familiar passages take on fresh depth and clarity. I found myself seeing stories I've known for years in completely new ways.*

*What I especially love is that each chapter ends with simple, practical action steps. This isn't just something you read and move on from—it's something that invites you to respond and apply what God is highlighting in your own life.*

*If you're looking for a devotional that's thoughtful, honest, and deeply grounding, I can't recommend this one enough.*

## Marc Walker
Husband, Girl Dad, Business Owner, Ministry Leader, Long Time Friend, EPIC Bro.

*Does the world really need another devotional book? After reading this one, I believe so. The blend of Scripture, devotional, and activation shines a new light on the book of Luke. You may even see yourself in the Gospels more than you ever imagined. Personal, profound, and worth a spot in your library. In other words, this is really good stuff.*

## Tim Walker
Father, Editor, Author, Writer, EPIC Bro.

*I've known Mark Brague for 35+ years. We've served together as ministry partners for a long time having traveled all over the world. The closer I've gotten to him, the more I love him. Mark is one of the greatest Christian men I know. He's sincere, real, a man, a real masculine godly man, he is seasoned, and he has learned how to truly walk with God and love people. He wrote this book and I believe it will help everyone who reads it to become like him, a true follower of Jesus, one who walks with God and loves people.*

## Chuck Ramsey
Lead Pastor at Restoration Church

*Mark has written us an uncommon devotional for the common man. His insights are real, spirit-led, and lived out. I believe every person can relate to Mark's real life applications. As we "listen" through Dr. Luke's amazing narrative, Mark Brague encourages us to expect the voice of God, to me specifically. This is not just God's voice to a people, or a generation. It is His voice to me. Thank you Mark for encouraging us to listen for the Counselor's voice as God's supernatural word provides the guardrails for living the Christian life without regret.*

## Peter Sorensen
Husband, Father, Christian Leader, CEO, EPIC Bro.

*This book reads like a quiet conversation with a trusted friend. One who knows the Scriptures deeply, loves God sincerely, and has learned to listen for the Spirit in the ordinary and unexpected moments of life. With humility and reverence, the author invites us into familiar passages of Luke's Gospel and helps us see them with fresh eyes. His reflections are honest, pastoral, and deeply human, drawing thoughtful connections between doubt, surrender, and our own daily choice to trust God when His plans don't look like ours.*

*What sets this work apart is not only its biblical insight, but the character of the man who wrote it. These pages are shaped by a life lived before God—marked by faith, obedience, and a genuine love for truth. Like Mary's simple yet courageous words, "Be it unto me as You have said," this book calls the reader toward a posture of surrender and trust, reminding us that God is good, His purposes are sure, and His grace is more than enough.*

*This is not just a book to be read, but one to be prayed through. It will stir your heart, steady your faith, and gently lead you back to wonder, gratitude, and confidence in the God who keeps His promises.*

Felix Mendez
Husband, Father, Servant for God, EPIC Bro.

This book is dedicated to my significantly better half, Gwen. Thank you for all the ways you love our family and invest yourself, with intention, in those around you. Thank you for choosing to believe the best of me, always. Without your love and capacity to extend grace and forgiveness, I would not be who I am today. Your love has made me a better man, father, and husband.

I would also like to dedicate the book to my sons, Elijah and Noah. If you two are a reflection and product of how we raised you, I know your mother and I did something right.

To their wives, Kasey and Reed, for the way you choose to love, honor and respect our sons. For the way you chase God and stretch yourselves to be the best versions of yourselves, we could not love you more. It's simply not possible. Period.

# CONTENTS

# foreword

There are books that are written to teach, books written to persuade, and books written to inspire. This one was written to listen.

I have watched Mark listen for most of his life—long before this devotional ever took shape. He has listened to people in moments of joy and grief. He listened to questions spoken out loud, and doubts whispered quietly, and to God in seasons when the answers felt clear and in seasons when they did not. Listening has never been a technique for him; it has been a posture of the heart.

Mark calls himself a former pastor, and that title matters to him. It matters because this book is not written from a place of performance or polish. It is written from lived experience. From wrestling. From unlearning. From choosing his sonship over image and faithfulness over certainty. Walking away from a formal role did not diminish his calling—it refined it. What remained for Mark was not a position, but a passion: to know Jesus more deeply and to invite others to do the same without hiding who they really are.

Listening through Luke was born out of that passion for real transparency. Luke's Gospel is uniquely attentive—attentive to voices often overlooked, to stories told with care, to the humanity of Jesus and the humanity of those He encountered. As Mark spent time in Luke, he wasn't searching for clever insights or quick applications. He was listening. And in that listening, he found himself invited again and again to slow down, to notice, and to respond honestly to what surfaced.

I have seen how this process has shaped him. There were mornings when the words he read unsettled him before they ever comforted him. There were evenings when conversations spilled over because what he was reflecting on could not stay neatly on the page.

This devotional is not the result of having everything figured out; it is the fruit of being willing to stay present, even when the text pressed close to tender places. I personally witnessed how he could write what inspired him while reading Luke, but as God breathed on his writing, he could not read it out loud without being emotionally moved. Listening moved him, and I believe listening will move you, too.

That is what makes this book an invitation rather than an instruction manual. Mark does not ask you to listen like he listens. He simply invites you to listen—truly listen—to Jesus as the gospel of Luke presents Him, and to pay attention to what that listening stirs within you. There is space here for questions. There is a daily action step to follow based on what you hear while Listening through Luke. There is room for doubt. And there is grace for the reader who comes tired, curious, hopeful, or unsure.

As Mark's wife, I can say this: the same honesty you will encounter in these pages is the honesty he strives to live. This book reflects his belief that faith is not weakened by transparency. Rather, it is strengthened by it. That God meets us not when we perform well, but when we show up fully ourselves...... listening.

My hope for you, the reader, is that Listening through Luke becomes a companion rather than a challenge—something that meets you where you are and gently encourages you to listen a little more closely. Not just to the words on the page, but to the voice of God that still speaks with compassion, clarity, and love.

May you find, as Mark has, that listening changes everything.

## Gwen Brague, Wife

Best-selling and award-winning author of *The Beautiful Ugly Truth* and *The Beautiful Ugly Truth Bible Study*

Co-founder of Reconnecting Lives
Life and Marriage Coach

# preface

This book was not planned. It came about quite organically, actually. I spent a year on a journey with some of the best EPIC brothers anyone could ever ask for. EPIC is a discipleship ministry of my home church, Restoration Church in North Atlanta. It stands for Experiential - Purposeful - Impactful - Christ-Centered. Our focus was on the Prophetic and coming to an understanding of how we, as individuals, hear what it is God is saying.

At one point in our journey together, we would read a chapter in the Bible a day, then share with the group what it was the Lord highlighted to us. Most days, I would get to the end of the exercise, knowing what I was reading back to myself did not come from my own thoughts. I could not read the writings to my wife without weeping. It became our morning routine. I would read, write then weep as I shared with Gwen what the Spirit had said. It was a sweet time of spiritual and emotional intimacy. I began receiving some positive feedback from the EPIC group. They felt strongly it was of a prophetic nature and encouraged me to continue compiling the writings. As I continued to listen and write, I felt some of the insights the Spirit showed me were not typical and were worth sharing outside of my small circle of brothers.

After much prayer and listening, here we are. This book is not intended to be a deep or complete theological work, although there is some theology mixed in. Nor is it an exegetical breakdown of each chapter, although you may find some exegesis sprinkled in. It is simply what I believe the Spirit was highlighting to me and saying in the moments as I would read and write.

My prayer is, through my writings, you would be inspired to read and listen for yourself what it is the Spirit says to you.

commit

The best way to approach *Listening Through Luke* and experience its full impact is to take it slowly, one chapter at a time, allowing each passage of Luke to guide its corresponding reflection. While only portions of each chapter are included in this book, you're encouraged to read the entire chapter in your own Bible and then return to the reflection space to process and respond.

Commit to 30 minutes a day without rushing. There is no timetable and certainly no challenge to finishing quickly. Those closest to me know I don't like games or contests, especially when it comes to spiritual matters.

The Spirit works on His time table. Not ours.

In fact, as I was journeying through Luke, there are some chapters so full, it took me more than one day to hear, let alone process what God was highlighting to the point where I could write a reflection.

So, sit with it. Take your time. God is always speaking. Allow yourself the grace to tune in and hear what the Spirit is saying to you.

At the end of each Reflection, we have built in some space for you to fill in with your own reflection and prayer. Write down what it is the Spirit said or highlighted to you. What section of the chapter stood out to you? Write it down. Maybe the Spirit will show you a picture, or an image may come to mind. Write it down. Maybe you will be reminded of a personal moment of your own that connects to the chapter. Maybe the Spirit will remind you of another story Jesus told. Write it down.

There are no rules. Just read, be open and write. You may be surprised as to what the Spirit says and how He says it.

Finish with the "Today I will' activation. Put into practice the things the Spirit says to you each day and see if you don't find yourself in divine encounters along the way.

# luke 1

## The Birth of Jesus Foretold

26 In the sixth month of Elizabeth's pregnancy, God sent the angel Gabriel to Nazareth, a town in Galilee, 27 to a virgin pledged to be married to a man named Joseph, a descendant of David. The virgin's name was Mary. 28 The angel went to her and said, "Greetings, you who are highly favored! The Lord is with you."

29 Mary was greatly troubled at his words and wondered what kind of greeting this might be. 30 But the angel said to her, "Do not be afraid, Mary; you have found favor with God. 31 You will conceive and give birth to a son, and you are to call him Jesus. 32 He will be great and will be called the Son of the Most High. The Lord God will give him the throne of his father David, 33 and he will reign over Jacob's descendants forever; his kingdom will never end."

34 "How will this be," Mary asked the angel, "since I am a virgin?"

35 The angel answered, "The Holy Spirit will come on you, and the power of the Most High will overshadow you. So the holy one to be born will be called[b] the Son of God. 36 Even Elizabeth your relative is going to have a child in her old age, and she who was said to be unable to conceive is in her sixth month. 37 For no word from God will ever fail."

38 "I am the Lord's servant," Mary answered. "May your word to me be fulfilled." Then the angel left her.

# Luke 1 Reflection

**"Be it unto me."**

Wow! Luke wastes no time getting to the meat of the story.

He starts with Zechariah and Elizabeth who are old and advanced in years. They have never conceived and have been praying for a child. Gabriel shows up to tell Zechariah the Lord has heard their prayer. The angel paints a picture of this baby. He tells them how they need to raise him. He says many will rejoice because of this baby. He tells Zechariah the baby is pivotal in the Messianic Narrative. Something Zechariah is familiar with since he is a Jewish priest. Gabriel talks about the awesome things this baby will do and how he will impact all of history!

Think about this. Zechariah and Elizabeth's prayers have been heard. Not only have they been heard, but they have been answered in spectacular fashion! Gabriel is dispatched from heaven to personally deliver the news to Zechariah. What a confirmation! But Zechariah is afraid and doubts. The thing he has been praying for is here yet he is afraid and doubts.

It's easy to read the passage and be confused by the lack of faith in Zechariah. I mean, c'mon man! Your prayers are being answered. After sitting with this for a while, I began to wonder how many times I, too, have prayed for something and God answered my prayer.

Only, I didn't like the way He answered it.
Only, I wanted it to look another way.
Only, it didn't fit into the comfortable life I had always imagined.
Only, the answer was 'no,' and I was angry because I thought I knew what was best for my life.

Have you ever been there? I suspect you have because you are human, like me.

You have this idea. This goal. This ideal thing you have dreamed up, and you are praying specifically. You believe this scenario would make you happy or would cause you to feel secure or complete. You may feel as though your idea was given to you by God himself!

But God gives you something different.

Not because He didn't hear your prayers or He doesn't care about you. It's quite the opposite, actually. He wants the very best for you. His best for you is better than anything you could have ever imagined or asked for, or dreamed up all on your own.

Paul tells us, in Ephesians, "God is able to do exceedingly abundantly above all we are able to ask or think."

Whatever I have dreamed up......
    God wants to do more.

Whatever I have thought about ......
    God's thoughts are higher than mine.

Whatever I have imagined .....
    God is more imaginative.

Or maybe, the thing I have dreamed up would lead to bad things in my life, and in His Sovereignty, God sees it and says "no" to my prayer because He has something better.

Then there's Mary.

She is literally minding her own business, and Gabriel pays her a visit to announce she will become pregnant.

I was not there at the time, and I am not a betting man. But I would be willing to place odds saying Mary was probably not praying to become pregnant. At least not the way Gabriel described it.

Given the culture of the day, why would anybody pray such a thing?

She has some questions for Gabriel, which is understandable, to say the least. It will clearly cause people to make assumptions. It will likely cause people to make accusations. It probably wasn't her idea of how her life would take shape. But ultimately, God gives her the grace she needs, and she receives it with the timeless passage, "Be it unto me as you have said."

Zechariah finally came around to God's plan, too. He needed some 'quiet time'. But he got there.

The reality is sometimes we pray, and things turn out differently than what we had hoped for. Sometimes we aren't praying at all, and life brings us a surprise.

It's moments like these when we have choices to make. We can choose to believe God is good or He is not. We can choose to believe He desires the very best for us, or He does not. Depending upon our circumstances, these choices are made daily. Sometimes moment-by-moment.

These are choices we must make intentionally.
> These are thoughts we must choose on purpose.
>> These are thoughts and decisions made purposefully in our brain, shifting and calming our emotions allowing us to see things differently.

When faced with difficulty or disappointment, if we don't choose trust, we can end up frustrated and doubting asking whether God is good. But if we choose to trust Him, it allows us to relax and say, 'I'm not sure what is happening in my life right now. This is not what I wanted or how I envisioned it, but 'Be it unto me as you have said'"

So, what will your posture with God be today?
> Trusting or doubting?
>> Faith or unbelief?
>>> God is good, or God doesn't even see me?

luke 1

# My Prayer

*Father,*

*I choose to trust You today. Cause faith to rise in me. Allow me the grace to lean into the fact that You are good and You want the best for me. I cannot see what You see. I do not know what You know. Yet I know You have plans for me. Plans that are good and for my betterment. I am choosing to trust You. 'Be it unto me as you have said.'*

*Amen*

## What is the Spirit saying to You?

Your Reflection

_______________________________________________

_______________________________________________

_______________________________________________

_______________________________________________

Your Prayer

_______________________________________________

_______________________________________________

_______________________________________________

_______________________________________________

Today I will _______________________________________

# luke 2

## The Birth of Jesus

1 In those days Caesar Augustus issued a decree that a census should be taken of the entire Roman world. 2 (This was the first census that took place while[a] Quirinius was governor of Syria.) 3 And everyone went to their own town to register.

4 So Joseph also went up from the town of Nazareth in Galilee to Judea, to Bethlehem the town of David, because he belonged to the house and line of David. 5 He went there to register with Mary, who was pledged to be married to him and was expecting a child. 6 While they were there, the time came for the baby to be born, 7 and she gave birth to her firstborn, a son. She wrapped him in cloths and placed him in a manger, because there was no guest room available for them.

8 And there were shepherds living out in the fields nearby, keeping watch over their flocks at night. 9 An angel of the Lord appeared to them, and the glory of the Lord shone around them, and they were terrified. 10 But the angel said to them, "Do not be afraid. I bring you good news that will cause great joy for all the people. 11 Today in the town of David a Savior has been born to you; he is the Messiah, the Lord. 12 This will be a sign to you: You will find a baby wrapped in cloths and lying in a manger."

13 Suddenly a great company of the heavenly host appeared with the angel, praising God and saying,

14 "Glory to God in the highest heaven,  and on earth peace to those on whom his favor rests."

15 When the angels had left them and gone into heaven, the shepherds said to one another, "Let's go to Bethlehem and see this thing that has happened, which the Lord has told us about."

16 So they hurried off and found Mary and Joseph, and the baby, who was lying in the manger. 17 When they had seen him, they spread the word concerning what had been told them about this child, 18 and all

who heard it were amazed at what the shepherds said to them. 19 But Mary treasured up all these things and pondered them in her heart. 20 The shepherds returned, glorifying and praising God for all the things they had heard and seen, which were just as they had been told.

## The Shepherds Fields of Bethlehem

It is hard for me to read this account without remembering my trip to Israel.

It was the Fall of 2019. We went to some amazing places and learned surprising things. The Shepherds' Fields of Bethlehem was one site which shook all of us. I had never heard of these fields until our trip. I will never forget it.

Right outside Bethlehem are fields and for centuries were tended by specific shepherds. They were Levitical Shepherds. These shepherds were tasked to raise sheep specifically for sacrifice. For centuries, Jews would pass through Bethlehem on their way up to their annual trip to Jerusalem for Passover. Rather than bring their sacrifice, they would purchase a lamb without spot or blemish. Here, in the Shepherds' Fields of Bethlehem.

I noticed a difference immediately. During our stay in Israel, we had seen shepherds leading their sheep through the desert up and down rugged dangerous mountainsides. Yes. They still do that! But these fields were terraced with lush flat places for the sheep to graze. These terraces were fenced off with knee-high walls built of desert stone. No telling how many centuries ago those walls were built. And there they stood. The terraces and walls were there so the sheep, intended for sacrifice, would not fall or injure themselves, causing a 'spot or blemish'.

As we listened to our guide that day, we learned there was a single birthing place for all of the lambs being born in these fields. When a ewe was ready to give birth, she would be taken to this structure and await the arrival of the new lamb. Upon birth, the newborn would be immediately 'wrapped tightly in cloth' so as not to cause injury. They would then be 'placed in a manger', a feeding trough, elevated above the floor to not be accidentally stepped on by the other livestock damaging them and making them unusable for sacrifice.

What?! I was stunned as I was hearing all about the history of this amazing place.

How did I not know? The prophetic implications and parallels made the hair on my arms stand up straight!

But it got even better!

*The Angel appears to the shepherds and says, "For there is born to you this day in the city of David a Savior, who is Christ the Lord. And this will be the sign to you: You will find a Babe wrapped in swaddling clothes, lying in a manger." Luke 2:11-12 NIV*

This passage has been quoted in every Christmas production I have ever attended in my entire life. The same is probably true for you as well. But I never noticed an important detail. The angel didn't tell them the exact location of the birth of this baby. The angel just said, "You will find a baby wrapped in cloth lying in a manger."

Notice, the shepherds didn't need to go searching. They didn't go door to door. They were not confused as to the baby's whereabouts. Nope! Those shepherds knew exactly where to go.

They went directly to the one birthing place where, for centuries, lamb after lamb after lamb had been born. Wrapped in cloth and laid in a manger.

Can you imagine what kind of night those shepherds must have had?

The Bible simply says 'they hurried off". It had to have been a bit more dramatic than that, though. Right? Try to envision the shepherd's experience of the night.

They were simply minding their business. Tending to their sheep. When suddenly an angel of the Lord shows up and lights up the darkness like white hot spotlights! If you've ever been in the desert you know how dark it is! The shepherds must have been shielding their eyes from the instant brightness. The angel announces the coming of the Messiah. As if that's not enough, an angel choir shows up to sing praises to God, for crying out loud!

As suddenly as they arrived, they are gone. The bright lights fade back into the night sky. And just like that, the shepherds are once again alone in the dark of the desert night. Standing motionless. Afraid to move. Staring at each other. Slow blinking in disbelief. Then, as if on cue, they simultaneously break off into a full sprint!

After all, these were Jewish boys who had heard the stories of Messiah who was to come and save them. Their whole lives, they had been told these stories by their fathers, and their fathers fathers.

Their minds must have been racing faster than their feet …

Could it be?
> The Savior?
> > The long prophesied Messiah?

They finally arrive at the birthing place. The one place where lambs meant for sacrifice had been born for centuries. They must have awkwardly come bursting into the serene Nativity scene. From full sprint to dead stop in a second. Breathing heavily from the run while their hearts pounded with anticipation.

And there He was.
> There. He. Was.
> > Just as the Angel had said.
> > > "Wrapped in swaddling clothes, lying in a manger."

They knew full well who He was. As the story spread, the entire region learned this was no ordinary lamb who was a worthy sacrifice for one man's sin for one year. No! This was the 'Lamb of God' who was worthy to be the sacrifice for every man! Not only for one year but for eternity!

At Jesus' baptism, years later, John the Baptist confirms the truth of how the story unfolded that eventful night in the Shepherds' Fields of Bethlehem by announcing Jesus to the world by saying, "Behold! The Lamb of God! Who takes away the sin of the world!"

As I stood there on the outskirts of those fields in stunned silence, I began to weep. Even as I am weeping now at the very thought of it. The reality of who Jesus is and what He accomplished is overwhelming. His gift of Grace and Mercy renewing every morning, which allows me to live freely and unafraid of the Father. His payment for my sin, which I could never have paid on my own, allows me to live without feeling as though I need to earn His approval or try to be good enough.

Saying "Thank You" seems small in comparison to His gift to us. Beyond gratitude, I have nothing else. Live in His Grace today. It is as real today as it was centuries ago on that night in the Shepherds' Fields of Bethlehem.

Receive it.

    Accept it.

        You didn't earn it.

        You can't make it go away.

# My Prayer

*Father,*

*My heart is overwhelmed with Your goodness. My mind cannot fully comprehend the work You did by coming as a baby and dying as Messiah. Sometimes, I am in awe, and I have nothing profound to express to You except to say, "Thank You". Thank You for Your Grace and Mercy. Thank You for making it  new every morning. Thank You for loving me the way You do. I sure do need it.*

*Amen*

**What is the Spirit saying to You?**

Your Reflection

_______________________________________________

_______________________________________________

_______________________________________________

Your Prayer

_______________________________________________

_______________________________________________

_______________________________________________

Today I will _______________________________________

# luke 3

## John the Baptist Prepares the Way

1 In the fifteenth year of the reign of Tiberius Caesar—when Pontius Pilate was governor of Judea, Herod tetrarch of Galilee, his brother Philip tetrarch of Iturea and Traconitis, and Lysanias tetrarch of Abilene— 2 during the high-priesthood of Annas and Caiaphas, the word of God came to John son of Zechariah in the wilderness. 3 He went into all the country around the Jordan, preaching a baptism of repentance for the forgiveness of sins. 4 As it is written in the book of the words of Isaiah the prophet:

"A voice of one calling in the wilderness, 'Prepare the way for the Lord, make straight paths for him.

5 Every valley shall be filled in, every mountain and hill made low. The crooked roads shall become straight, the rough ways smooth.

6 And all people will see God's salvation.'"[a]

7 John said to the crowds coming out to be baptized by him, "You brood of vipers! Who warned you to flee from the coming wrath? 8 Produce fruit in keeping with repentance. And do not begin to say to yourselves, 'We have Abraham as our father.' For I tell you that out of these stones God can raise up children for Abraham. 9 The ax is already at the root of the trees, and every tree that does not produce good fruit will be cut down and thrown into the fire."

10 "What should we do then?" the crowd asked.

11 John answered, "Anyone who has two shirts should share with the one who has none, and anyone who has food should do the same."

12 Even tax collectors came to be baptized. "Teacher," they asked, "what should we do?"

13 "Don't collect any more than you are required to," he told them.

14 Then some soldiers asked him, "And what should we do?"

He replied, "Don't extort money and don't accuse people falsely—be content with your pay."

15 The people were waiting expectantly and were all wondering in their hearts if John might possibly be the Messiah. 16 John answered them all, "I baptize you with[b] water. But one who is more powerful than I will come, the straps of whose sandals I am not worthy to untie. He will baptize you with[c] the Holy Spirit and fire. 17 His winnowing fork is in his hand to clear his threshing floor and to gather the wheat into his barn, but he will burn up the chaff with unquenchable fire." 18 And with many other words John exhorted the people and proclaimed the good news to them.

19 But when John rebuked Herod the tetrarch because of his marriage to Herodias, his brother's wife, and all the other evil things he had done, 20 Herod added this to them all: He locked John up in prison.

## What Should I Do?

It seems as though all types of people were coming out to see John to be baptized. Everyday people. Tax collectors. Even Soldiers. All being lit up and scolded by John with his fiery brand of preaching. All kinds of people were coming to him and thought He might be the long-awaited Messiah.

He tells them the 'Axe is already at the root" - "every tree that does not bear fruit will be chopped down and thrown into the fire" alluding to their eternal future. It is a blistering and accusatory type of message! A message of correction. A call for repentance and change. Surprisingly, most of the people are not offended. Instead, they ask the question, "What should we do?"

He responds by calling them a 'Brood of Vipers"! He tells them to share with one another and feed one another. He tells the Tax Collectors to stop taking more than necessary. He tells the soldiers to stop lying and cheating.

The word of what was happening had made its way throughout the land to the degree to which it caught King Herod's attention. But when John called out Herod for marrying his brother's wife, Herod didn't ask, "What should I do?" Instead, he chose offense and threw John into prison.

Herod's lack of self-awareness is glaring to everyone except Herod himself. Because you can't be self-aware if you're self-absorbed. Herod is a mess.

In reading the story, I would never identify with Herod. I would definitely be one of the humble people who asked, "What should I do?" Right?

If I'm being honest,  as I look back on my life, there are moments when I wasn't super obedient to the things of the Spirit either.

I am reminded of a specific event.

Years ago, my wife and I visited a church at the invitation of some close friends. It was known to be a prophetic church, and we found ourselves sitting in a room with some prophetically gifted people. The idea was we would circle up. They would pray over us then share with us what the Spirit was saying to them on our behalf. What nobody knew was I was caught in a secret sin loop.

Secret sin. It's a feeling of helplessness. I didn't like it. I wanted to break the cycle, but I didn't know how to do it without crushing my wife.

There we were, in a little circle of prophetic people, all charged up and ready to hear from the Lord. I was terrified at the prospect of being exposed, yet there was little I could do to finagle my way out of the moment.

There I sat. In a circle of people I did not know. Slow breathing to fend off the anxiety. Looking cool but squirming on the inside. Terrified of what might be said. The gentleman who began spoke in general terms. He alluded to how I should love my wife with purity and with holiness.

I will never know if the Spirit told him anything specific about my secrets. My sense is the Spirit showed him some things, but he was kind enough not to expose me. I was relieved he did not completely blow me up right then and there.

After he spoke the truth with kindness and grace as the Spirit gave him insight, what was my response? Did I humbly ask, "What must I do?"

No.

I got mad. I didn't say anything to him or the Prophetic team that night, but as soon as I could escape the room, I railed about how horribly

     LISTENING THROUGH LUKE

wrong the guy was. "What kind of wing-nuts do they have around here?" I went on about how off base and offensive he was.

Nothing was further from the truth. The man was a gentleman. He was kind. Furthermore, he was right.

There I was. Being gently convicted by the Spirit, not allowing my heart to soften. Rather than receive His correction, I chose offense and metaphorically, threw the Holy Spirit into 'prison' because I didn't want to hear it. Because I didn't want to deal with it.

A couple of years later, God led us to a place where all the secrets came out. God led us through the process with such kindness. It wasn't easy. I had hurt my wife. I had to make amends. I had a lot of trust to earn back from her, and I will be forever grateful she chose the hard work of forgiveness.

Now I can look back and see my pride.
> I see how self-absorbed I was.
> Just like Herod.

Luke doesn't end the chapter there. He ends the chapter with the genealogy of Jesus. It seems random. Why would Luke bother to include the information? It seems out of place until you realize who is in His lineage.

You would expect perfection. After all, this is Jesus. Surely he comes from a stellar lineage. But this list is not perfect. Some of the people listed are not stellar. Not even close.

Yes, there are saints. But there are also sinners
> Yes, there are kings, but there are also prostitutes.

There are heroes of the faith and people who completely failed. There are murderers, adulterers, and idolaters and everyone in between.

Jesus is perfect. Everyone else is not. Yet He gave Himself for all of us, which tells me He gets it. He is acquainted with sin. He is not shocked by failure. He can identify brokenness. He is familiar with heartache.

That comforts me. On the days when I look and feel more like Herod than Jesus, He has grace for me. Not because I deserve it. Quite the opposite, actually. I, in no way, deserve it. But I need it. And He gives it.

# My Prayer

*Father,*

*When I lean on my own abilities to be good enough, remind me I am more like Herod than Jesus. Remind me Jesus loves me just the same. Help me stay close to You in all things. Surround me with people who care about me enough to speak into my life with love and bring me back in from the edges. May I be soft and receptive to the convicting voice of your Holy Spirit.*

*Amen*

## What is the Spirit saying to You?

Your Reflection

_________________________________________________

_________________________________________________

_________________________________________________

_________________________________________________

Your Prayer

_________________________________________________

_________________________________________________

_________________________________________________

_________________________________________________

Today I will _____________________________________

# luke 4

## Jesus Is Tested in the Wilderness

1 Jesus, full of the Holy Spirit, left the Jordan and was led by the Spirit into the wilderness, 2 where for forty days he was tempted[a] by the devil. He ate nothing during those days, and at the end of them he was hungry.

3 The devil said to him, "If you are the Son of God, tell this stone to become bread."

4 Jesus answered, "It is written: 'Man shall not live on bread alone.'[b]"

5 The devil led him up to a high place and showed him in an instant all the kingdoms of the world. 6 And he said to him, "I will give you all their authority and splendor; it has been given to me, and I can give it to anyone I want to. 7 If you worship me, it will all be yours."

8 Jesus answered, "It is written: 'Worship the Lord your God and serve him only.'[c]"

9 The devil led him to Jerusalem and had him stand on the highest point of the temple. "If you are the Son of God," he said, "throw yourself down from here. 10 For it is written:

"'He will command his angels concerning you

    to guard you carefully;

11 they will lift you up in their hands,

    so that you will not strike your foot against a stone.'[d]"

12 Jesus answered, "It is said: 'Do not put the Lord your God to the test.'[e]"

13 When the devil had finished all this tempting, he left him until an opportune time.

# Luke 4 Reflections

## The Thing About the Wilderness

Many times, as believers, if something doesn't go the way we want; business struggles, relationships are tough, etc, we label it as a wilderness season. Sometimes we take that on and personalize it. We figure we are experiencing a wilderness season because of a failure. Or, perhaps, we have displeased God somehow, and we are being punished. Other times, we refuse to take any accountability whatsoever and blame it on the enemy. Because this tough spot, this wilderness season, this heartbreak, is definitely outside of anything God would do or allow.

Or is it?

Right after Jesus was baptized, the scripture tells us He was led by the Spirit into the wilderness to be tempted by the devil.

Wait a minute! Led by the Spirit? For the expressed purpose of being tempted?

Yup.

And if the Spirit will lead Jesus into the wilderness immediately after saying, "This is my Son in whom I am well pleased", will He not, in His sovereignty, lead us as well into sticky or tough situations?

Yes. I think so. Sometimes.

The Spirit will lead us into the wilderness for seasons of growth and pruning. Hebrews 5 tells us Jesus learned obedience through the things He suffered. If it was good enough for Jesus then it's good enough for you and me.

Additionally, the world is broken and not fair. Sometimes wilderness seasons simply come. Hard things happen outside of our control.

Sickness comes. Unexpected loss happens. And let's be honest. We are more than capable of creating some of our trouble all by ourselves. We can blame the devil all we want to. But you know as well as I do. There are some moments when the devil didn't need to help us. We did it all by ourselves. Maybe you can identify. I'm suspecting you can.

No matter the reason for the tough season we are in, they are real and they are not easy.

The longer I live, I find myself leaning into what Paul said in Philippians. "I have learned to be content whatever the circumstances." Philippians 4:11

I'll be honest. I used to not like that passage, because when life kicks me in the pants, my first instinct is not to be holy. My first instinct is to feel sorry for myself and lean into my broken nature. I read that passage, and my attitude sounds something like,

"Good for you, Paul!
      Ya got it all figured out, do ya?
            I'm super happy for you......NOT!"

But somewhere along the line, the Holy Spirit showed me Paul is not bragging here. He is not saying he is better than you or me. It is actually a humble confession of quite the opposite.

He writes he had to *learn* to be content. Which means at some point, he didn't *know* how to be content. You only have to learn things you don't know. During the learning process, you try and fail. A lot.

The reality brought me a great amount of peace. It brought me peace, because Paul wrote 2/3 of the New Testament and is the closest thing to Jesus Jr. we've ever had. And if he had to learn how to be content, then I am empowered to not beat myself up too bad when my attitude makes it clear I still have some learning to do.

Because Jesus has Grace for me even when I'm being rotten. Probably

             LISTENING THROUGH LUKE

especially when I'm being rotten. Because if Grace doesn't apply when I don't deserve it, then it isn't Grace. That would be something else. But it would not be Grace.

Grace is the undeserved favor of God. Which means if I can ever be good enough to deserve it, I would be disqualified from receiving it. Because He gives it to those who don't deserve it.

Read the last three sentences again.
      Slowly.
            Let it sink in.

By definition, I am not qualified to receive Grace unless I have screwed something up. Have you ever screwed something up? Congratulations! You qualify to receive His Grace.

Like Paul, I am learning to be content in all situations. Whether God has led me to a wilderness season for my own sanctification, or life is just being life, or I have caused my own trouble. I know He can use it all.

# My Prayer

*Father,*

*Help me to trust you and serve you even when things aren't good and I would rather they look different. Give me the grace and strength I need in the moments of life's hard places. Remind me You are good and You use all things to refine me. Remind me of the words I just wrote when my attitude is contrary to Your sovereignty.*

*Amen*

## What is the Spirit saying to You?

Your Reflection

_________________________________________________

_________________________________________________

_________________________________________________

_________________________________________________

Your Prayer

_________________________________________________

_________________________________________________

_________________________________________________

_________________________________________________

Today I will __________________________________________

# luke 5

## Jesus Calls His First Disciples

1 One day as Jesus was standing by the Lake of Gennesaret,[a] the people were crowding around him and listening to the word of God. 2 He saw at the water's edge two boats, left there by the fishermen, who were washing their nets. 3 He got into one of the boats, the one belonging to Simon, and asked him to put out a little from shore. Then he sat down and taught the people from the boat.

4 When he had finished speaking, he said to Simon, "Put out into deep water, and let down the nets for a catch."

5 Simon answered, "Master, we've worked hard all night and haven't caught anything. But because you say so, I will let down the nets."

# Luke 5 Reflection

## Belief and Doubt

I was drawn to the section where Jesus asks the disciples if they have caught anything. When the answer is 'no', Jesus recommends they toss their nets on the other side of the boat.

Peter replies by saying "Master, we've worked hard all night and haven't caught anything. But because you say so, I will let down the nets."
Luke 5:5

Clearly, there was doubt in Peter's mind. These guys were fishermen. Uneducated in the Torah, yes. But they knew how to fish. They knew throwing the nets on the other side of the boat was going to make little to no difference whatsoever. They doubted the results would be any different.

They doubted. Not only on this occasion. Peter and most of the other disciples scattered like the wind during the Crucifixion. John the Baptist doubted when he was in prison and sent a few of his disciples to ask Jesus if He was actually the Messiah or should they be looking for another.

Doubts are a part of the human experience. Doubting is quite normal and common to us all. It's not doubting that's the problem. The problem is we tend to believe our doubts. Rather than pressing through and continuing with simple obedience, we choose to stop and believe our doubts. Similarly, we tend to doubt our beliefs.

We pray and believe for healing.
>But we doubt it will happen

We pray and believe for a breakthrough in a relationship.
>But we doubt the other person will ever change.

We pray and believe for finances to open up.
>But doubt we will ever see anything beyond a paycheck-to-pay check life.

On and on and on. The cycle continues. Believing our doubts and doubting our beliefs.

What would it look like if we made a decision to believe our beliefs and doubt our doubts? Not to say we would never have another doubting thought run through our minds. I heard an old preacher say, "You can't control what birds fly overhead. But you can sure enough control which ones make a nest in your hair."

What if, when the next doubting thought comes, rather than agree with it, we choose to say to ourselves, "I doubt that". I think our lives would look tremendously different. Maybe not all at once. But over time, our lives would take a different shape and feel because our lives are shaped by our thoughts. I'm not talking about a magic quick fix for all of life's issues. I'm talking about the fact that our emotions are shaped by our thinking. How you feel about something is directly connected to how you think about it.

Good emotion? There's a good thought first.

Negative emotion? There's a negative thought behind it.

Most often, we make our decisions and choices based on our emotions and how we feel about something. If we have a negative thought pattern, it will produce a negative emotion. If we are stuck in a negative emotion, we will typically make a negative decision or choice.

     LISTENING THROUGH LUKE

Generally speaking, our lives are a cumulative product of our choices and decisions. There are always exceptions. I am not speaking about those who have been wounded or traumatized in some way and are true victims of somebody else's decisions. But generally speaking, our choices and decisions shape our lives. Even our decisions about how we respond to the trauma and wounds we were powerless to control have an effect on our lives.

Big decisions and small decisions. They all go into shaping our lives for the better or for the worse. Our life is a product of our choices and decisions. Our choices and decisions are typically driven by our emotions. Our emotions are shaped by what we choose to think.

How we choose to think is critical to the shape of our lives.

The reality is there is very little in life you can control.

You can't control the economy. You can't control your boss. You can't control traffic. You can't control your spouse (I don't recommend even trying) You think you can control your kids. And maybe you can until they are two. But if your kids are anything like my kids, when they are married with children of their own, they will tell you all the things they did behind your back when you were sure you were in firm control.

The only thing we truly have control over is our thinking. The problem is we seldom think about what we think about.

Most often, we are shaped as children into a pattern of thinking. We are shaped by trauma and pain. We make declarations and inner vows over ourselves which aren't always healthy. Due to coping mechanisms like these, we formulate limiting beliefs and thought patterns.

Thought patterns produce emotion. Emotion produces choices. Choices produce the quality of our reality. If left unchecked, negative or even destructive thinking can run wild without us even understanding what is happening. So, we have to dig deep. We have to uncover and expose the lies we have agreed with. We have to undo harmful inner vows.

We have to realize the most damaging and harmful things said to us are the things we say to ourselves. We have to think about what we are thinking about.

Biblical vocabulary for this is "take every thought captive and make it obedient to Christ"  - 2 Corinthians 10:5

So, will I go on doubting my beliefs and believing my doubts?
Or will I choose to believe my beliefs and doubt my doubts?

Back to Peter in the boat. He could have stopped with "we've been fishing all night." He was a fisherman. He had been at it all night. On the one hand, it looked obvious. But Peter took a moment. He chose his thinking.

The next time you have an opportunity to choose belief or doubt. Which will you choose?

# My Prayer

*Father,*

*Help me choose obedience to your word over my thoughts and life experience. Help me keep the perspective that You see it all, know it all, and want the very best for me. Help me choose to think that You are good and are for me in all things. Help me take a moment like Peter. Despite my experience and perspective, help me continue through with obedience and respond as Peter did: "Master, we've worked hard all night and haven't caught anything. But because you say so, I will let down the nets."*

*Amen*

**What is the Spirit saying to You?**

Your Reflection

_________________________________________

_________________________________________

_________________________________________

_________________________________________

Your Prayer

_________________________________________

_________________________________________

_________________________________________

_________________________________________

Today I will _______________________________

# luke 6

## Jesus Is Lord of the Sabbath

1 One Sabbath Jesus was going through the grainfields, and his disciples began to pick some heads of grain, rub them in their hands and eat the kernels. 2 Some of the Pharisees asked, "Why are you doing what is unlawful on the Sabbath?"

3 Jesus answered them, "Have you never read what David did when he and his companions were hungry? 4 He entered the house of God, and taking the consecrated bread, he ate what is lawful only for priests to eat. And he also gave some to his companions." 5 Then Jesus said to them, "The Son of Man is Lord of the Sabbath."

6 On another Sabbath he went into the synagogue and was teaching, and a man was there whose right hand was shriveled. 7 The Pharisees and the teachers of the law were looking for a reason to accuse Jesus, so they watched him closely to see if he would heal on the Sabbath. 8 But Jesus knew what they were thinking and said to the man with the shriveled hand, "Get up and stand in front of everyone." So he got up and stood there.

9 Then Jesus said to them, "I ask you, which is lawful on the Sabbath: to do good or to do evil, to save life or to destroy it?"

10 He looked around at them all, and then said to the man, "Stretch out your hand." He did so, and his hand was completely restored. 11 But the Pharisees and the teachers of the law were furious and began to discuss with one another what they might do to Jesus.

## The Misbehaving Jesus

Jesus doubles down on offending the Pharisees on the Sabbath. Part of me likes it when religious people are offended. Especially the Pharisees. Why were they always fighting against Jesus? It doesn't seem to make sense on the surface.

But when I take a step back, I can see where they were coming from. The Pharisees were, by and large, well intended. Of course, with everything, there are always bad apples. But generally, they were God loving and God fearing people who had given their lives to ministry and service.

The Pharisees were looking for the Messiah to come. They believed the Messiah would not come until the law was followed. The Pharisees believed  if they could manage to keep every law God gave in the Old Testament for a 24-hour Sabbath, that would prompt God to hasten sending the Messiah to Israel.

In fact, to help ensure no one broke a law, they came up with thousands more regulations to act as guardrails around the Torah in hopes that no one even came close to breaking the Law during that critical 24-hour period.

It is all they had been taught. They were taught by Godly men who mentored them and raised them in the tradition of the faith. With that in mind, I can understand their insistence on following the Law.

So, imagine the mental gymnastics their brains must have been going through. Here is the very Messiah they were praying for, looking for, hoping for, driving the people into legalism for. He is standing right there in front of them and He is the one who is BREAKING THE LAW!

What do you do when you find yourself in a place that feels contrary to everything you ever dreamed or planned for your life? How do I respond and react when I feel like Jesus should be doing something a particular way, but He is simply not cooperating?

What do you do when you have prayed for something and either your prayer apparently got lost in heaven or something happened contrary to what you prayed for?

Never mind the Pharisees. How is my attitude toward Jesus in those moments? I prayed so hard. I put so much energy into my faith to believe for whatever it is I have been contending for.

Am I angry? Am I disappointed?

It is in these painfully honest moments of self-reflection that I realize I have the capacity to be far more pharisaical than Christlike.

I can get there quickly.

Years ago, I was serving as a spiritual director for an organization that leads weekend retreats for college aged young adults and high school students. Months of planning meetings take place before each weekend. The leader of the weekend actually begins building their teams up to a year before the actual event. The detailed organization around every moment of the weekend is quite stunning. Literally, every word and moment is thought through and prayerfully considered.

These weekends are glorious.

This particular weekend was a young lady's weekend. One of the roles needing to be filled by volunteers involves being at the podium, reading letters and notes of encouragement to those attending the event. The team which had been assembled to fill that particular role had five or six young ladies. At least four of them had learning disabilities or challenges of one kind or another which made reading quite a challenge, let alone reading in front of people, which had to have led to additional nervousness among the team. These sweet young ladies knew their limitations, but said "yes" when they were asked to serve.

Well, the moment came for them to step up to the microphone and read their notes. I wish I could say they performed without a hitch. I wish I could say it was flawless and God miraculously gave them the ability to read without struggling. But, He didn't. It was painful to hear and awkward to watch. You could feel the tension in the room.

My mind immediately began asking questions.

> "Who thought it would be a good idea to ask these sweet girls to fill this particular role?"

> "There are plenty of other jobs to do which don't include reading publicly!"

> "Did the leaders even pray about it?"

These young ladies had to read publicly several times over the weekend. Each time was as disastrous as the first. I was sure the leadership team completely struck out on the whole 'let the Lord lead you' thing. I wasn't the only one. There was simply no way this made any sense at all. At least to us. At least from our perspective.

The weekend wraps up with the people who attended sharing something of their experience and what it meant to them.

There is no way any of us could have predicted it. There is no way we could have known it. But as those young ladies began to share, at least 10 or 12 of them said to the crowd that they, too, had reading or learning difficulties of some kind. They talked about how they felt as though their issue disqualified them from serving God. The sentiment was, "But if these girls can do it, then so can I!"

You just can't make this stuff up.

I sat in stunned silence as tears rolled down my face. Tears of joy. Tears of repentance over my critical attitude. God was in complete control and had an absolutely glorious plan despite my pharisaical posture on that particular weekend.

The reality is, Jesus rarely did things the way He was 'supposed' to. He came as a helpless baby when He was expected as a conquering King. He ate with sinners and tax collectors when He was supposed to avoid sinners. He broke the Jewish Laws all the time when keeping the Law was supposed to be the goal. He let his friend Lazarus die when it could have been avoided.

It's easy for us to read the Bible and, from our vantage point, wonder why Mary and Martha were mad at Jesus when He got there three days after Lazarus died. Did they not know Jesus was getting ready to raise their brother from the dead?

No, actually. They didn't.

The next time something is happening and you are sure Jesus is not a part of the equation ...

The next time it looks like Jesus has 'left the building' ...
       Leave room in your thinking...
          For this possibility.
              Jesus might be up to something glorious.

# My Prayer

*Father,*

*Help me. The next time You aren't doing what I think You should be doing, help me to leave space in my thinking to realize You might be up to something in my life. Help me remember Your plan is good. Your plan is perfect. Help me to remember up until this point in my life, there have been surprises and curveballs. None of which I would have chosen. But my life is richer, truer and more honest as a result. I would not trade it for the world. Help me to remember.*

*Amen*

## What is the Spirit saying to You?

Your Reflection

________________________________________

________________________________________

________________________________________

________________________________________

Your Prayer

________________________________________

________________________________________

________________________________________

________________________________________

Today I will _______________________________

# luke 7

## The Faith of the Centurion

1 When Jesus had finished saying all this to the people who were listening, he entered Capernaum. 2 There a centurion's servant, whom his master valued highly, was sick and about to die. 3 The centurion heard of Jesus and sent some elders of the Jews to him, asking him to come and heal his servant. 4 When they came to Jesus, they pleaded earnestly with him, "This man deserves to have you do this, 5 because he loves our nation and has built our synagogue." 6 So Jesus went with them.

He was not far from the house when the centurion sent friends to say to him: "Lord, don't trouble yourself, for I do not deserve to have you come under my roof. 7 That is why I did not even consider myself worthy to come to you. But say the word, and my servant will be healed. 8 For I myself am a man under authority, with soldiers under me. I tell this one, 'Go,' and he goes; and that one, 'Come,' and he comes. I say to my servant, 'Do this,' and he does it."

9 When Jesus heard this, he was amazed at him, and turning to the crowd following him, he said, "I tell you, I have not found such great faith even in Israel." 10 Then the men who had been sent returned to the house and found the servant well.

## The Forest For the Trees

The chapter opens with the story of the Centurion and his servant who is ill. The Centurion is not a religious man. He is certainly not a Jew, but he has heard the stories and understands Jesus is a miracle worker.

He accepts it. He receives it.

He has such confidence in Jesus's authority and ability he doesn't even ask for Jesus to come to his house. In fact, he says he is not worthy of it. He simply says, "Just say the word and my servant will be healed."

Later, Jesus is anointed by the sinful woman. Her level of gratitude compels her to wash Jesus's feet with her tears.

The Centurion's faith and the Sinful Woman's display of love toward Jesus are contrasted by the Pharisees who can't seem to get past their religion and traditions to see who Jesus is.

The Messiah. The very one whom they were looking for and dedicated their lives to is standing right there in front of them. But they are so tied up in their traditions and so locked into their teachings they can't see it.

When I first became a full-time vocational Pastor, I remember the sense of fulfillment and satisfaction. It was something I had longed for and even dreamed about. I had always struggled with being good enough and measuring up. But people were now calling me 'Pastor'.

Surely, I had arrived.
> Surely this proves my worth.
>> Surely this means I am good enough ... finally.

My wife and I dove headfirst into the deep end of ministry along with everything it entails. We sincerely loved the ministry life with all of its sacrifices and challenges. God was stretching us. We were growing. I was called. I was a minister of the Gospel.

I loved teaching and breaking down the word. I took great pride in making it applicable to the people under my care. Learning the Word. Studying the Word. Finding nuggets, like buried treasure, and sharing what I had found was exhilarating. It made me feel special. It made me feel smart. It made me feel worthy of the title of Pastor.

I started with every good intention, but after years of that cycle, it became more and more an exercise in measuring up once again. It devolved into me proving I was worthy of the title and position. I wasn't hooked on drugs. But I was addicted. Addicted to what people thought of me. Addicted to their words to me and their words about me. I didn't only want them to say good things about me. I needed them to.

I stopped studying and reading the Word for my own enrichment and personal relationship with Jesus and started spending time in the Word to write a message for others.

Find the principle. Find the pattern. Find the three words that rhyme. I had fallen into the trap.

My affirmation and validation wasn't coming from Father God.

It was coming from the people I was leading.
    It was coming from my title and position.

I wonder if that's what the Pharisees were dealing with in their hearts and minds as Jesus was literally walking the streets healing people and raising dead people to life.

I wonder if their sense of self-importance was blinding their ability to see the reality of what was happening in real time right there in front of them.

I wonder if their pride surrounding their titles and the things they had taught caused them to forget the very One about whom they were teaching.

Jesus didn't fit the principle. Jesus didn't fit the pattern. Jesus ruined their rhyme.

I wanted to be like the Centurion. Filled with raw faith. I wanted to be like the sinful woman, who was filled with such gratitude that her tears washed Jesus's feet. But I had become like the Pharisees. Working hard for the approval of others. My sense of validation was in my title and my ability. I couldn't see my validation was in Jesus. I couldn't see the forest for the trees.

Jesus was kind enough to wake me up and lead me home. Home to Him.

I still want to be accepted. I still want people to like me. I just don't need them to anymore.

Still, every so often, If I'm not careful to spend time with Jesus, that old addiction will rear its ugly head. And in those moments, I have to remind myself that my only source of unconditional acceptance, value and worth is in Jesus. It was always in Jesus. It will always be in Jesus.

# My Prayer

*Father,*

*May my heart always be to please you and not those around me. May my pursuit not be in titles or positions given by men. May my heart's desire be satisfied in who You say I am.*

*Forgiven*
*Son*
*Enough*

*Amen*

**What is the Spirit saying to You?**

Your Reflection

_____________________________________________

_____________________________________________

_____________________________________________

_____________________________________________

Your Prayer

_____________________________________________

_____________________________________________

_____________________________________________

_____________________________________________

Today I will _________________________________

# luke 8

## Jesus Raises a Dead Girl and Heals a Sick Woman

40 Now when Jesus returned, a crowd welcomed him, for they were all expecting him. 41 Then a man named Jairus, a synagogue leader, came and fell at Jesus' feet, pleading with him to come to his house 42 because his only daughter, a girl of about twelve, was dying.

As Jesus was on his way, the crowds almost crushed him. 43 And a woman was there who had been subject to bleeding for twelve years,[c] but no one could heal her. 44 She came up behind him and touched the edge of his cloak, and immediately her bleeding stopped.

45 "Who touched me?" Jesus asked.

When they all denied it, Peter said, "Master, the people are crowding and pressing against you."

46 But Jesus said, "Someone touched me; I know that power has gone out from me."

47 Then the woman, seeing that she could not go unnoticed, came trembling and fell at his feet. In the presence of all the people, she told why she had touched him and how she had been instantly healed. 48 Then he said to her, "Daughter, your faith has healed you. Go in peace."

# Luke 8 Reflection

## Jesus at Arms Length

What an action packed chapter.

Jesus tells the iconic Parable of the Sower. He talks about how nobody lights a lamp and hides it. He tells a storm to stop, and it does!

The disciples are in awe!

He delivers a demoniac who had been in bondage his whole life. This is the famous story where Jesus asks the demon its name, and it replies, "Legion". Apparently, there were a lot of demons in the man. They beg Jesus not to send them to the abyss. They beg to go into a herd of pigs nearby. The demons leave the man and enter the pigs, and the pigs run into the lake and drown!

What a day! What stood out to me was the next story in the chapter.

People had heard about the things Jesus had been doing. A crowd of people were there to greet Him on the shore when He arrived. The Bible says the crowd was nearly crushing Him.

Try to imagine the scene. People were everywhere. No doubt they were excited to see Him. Maybe they had pressing needs and were after Jesus to heal or fix whatever was wrong. Or maybe they were just curious and wanted to see Jesus for themselves.

While Jesus was making His way through the press of the crowd, the disciples were likely pushing people out of the way so He could pass. Amid the frenzy, a woman who had been struggling with an issue of blood for twelve years managed to fight her way through the press of the crowd. From the ground, she reached up and touched the hem of His robe.

It caused Jesus to stop and ask, "Who touched me?"

Even though we were just told the crowd was nearly crushing Him, the Bible says they all denied touching Him. What? Clearly, at least some of them had to have touched him. Either on purpose or maybe the crowd pushed them into Jesus. Yet they all denied touching Him. To be fair, I can understand the conflicted nature of the people that day. They wanted to be close to Jesus. But not too close. After all, Jesus had just delivered the man with a Legion of demons inside of him.

Slow down and replay this scenario in your mind.

Jesus simply spoke and a Legion of demons came out of a man. Not one demon. A legion. To heighten the drama, those demons chose to drown themselves in a herd of pigs rather than face Him!

Jesus also recently told a storm to sit down and shut up. Don't miss this. He talked to the wind! Only crazy people talk to the wind. Unless, of course, the wind obeys. Then they're not crazy. Then they have super-natural powers and are potentially dangerous to be around.

The people had heard the stories. The people were clamoring to see this man, and now this man has stopped in His tracks and has turned His steely gaze towards the people who have been pressing in. He wants to know, "Who touched me?"

What an intense moment it must have been.
What does He want?
What is He going to do?
Is He going to cause bad things to happen?
Are we the next group destined for a herd of pigs?
Is He going to expose me right here in front of everybody?

All of the people pressing in had their reasons. When asked about it, rather than press through their apprehensions and fears and make themselves vulnerable to Jesus, they were all content to keep Him at arm's length.

　　　　LISTENING THROUGH LUKE

All of them, except the woman who had reached the end of her rope and had literally nothing left except the hope that if she could get close enough to touch His garment, she could be healed.

She literally had nothing to lose. We are told in scripture that she had spent all of her money on Doctors and none of them could help her. She went for it. She pressed through the frenzy of the crowd. She pushed and fought her way through until she was close. She reached up. She touched Him. Her desperation caused power to leave Jesus's body and heal her.

After realizing she could not slip through the crowd undetected, and Jesus was asking questions, the Bible says she trembled as she stepped forward to confess it was she who had touched Him and that touch had healed her.

There she was. Helpless and vulnerable in front of Him, literally at His mercy. Which is exactly what she received. His mercy. His goodness and kindness.

My wife and I were able to visit that site a few years ago.
> The spot where Jesus walked.
>> The spot where the crowd was crushing in.
>>> The very spot where power left His body.

In the small town of Magdala, off the coast of the Sea of Galilee.

We stood on those very stones where that woman was healed. We stood on those very stones where power came from Jesus. We were all overcome with awe and emotion as we contemplated that reality. There were many tears shed and even deep groanings the day of our visit. Not because we were sad, but because the power that left Jesus's body 2,000 years ago is still somehow flowing. It is still somehow healing. Right there at that spot. You can feel it. You can sense it.

Because Jesus is that powerful. Because Jesus has that much authority.

Much like the Woman with the Issue of Blood, what we discovered that day in Magdala is that the only thing surpassing the level of Jesus's power and authority is the overwhelming measure of His mercy, goodness and kindness.

You can know it too. But you have to press through your fears and apprehensions. You have to be willing to risk it all to get close enough to Him to discover it for yourself.

They all touched Jesus that day. But only the *Woman with the Issue of Blood* was touched by Him.

# My Prayer

*Father,*

*May I never hold you at arm's length. May I always live in a posture of complete surrender to your power and authority because it is only then I am truly capable of receiving your love and kindness.*

*Amen*

## What is the Spirit saying to You?

Your Reflection

_______________________________________________

_______________________________________________

_______________________________________________

_______________________________________________

Your Prayer

_______________________________________________

_______________________________________________

_______________________________________________

_______________________________________________

Today I will _______________________________________________

# luke 9

## Jesus Sends Out the Twelve

1 When Jesus had called the Twelve together, he gave them power and authority to drive out all demons and to cure diseases, 2 and he sent them out to proclaim the kingdom of God and to heal the sick. 3 He told them: "Take nothing for the journey—no staff, no bag, no bread, no money, no extra shirt. 4 Whatever house you enter, stay there until you leave that town. 5 If people do not welcome you, leave their town and shake the dust off your feet as a testimony against them." 6 So they set out and went from village to village, proclaiming the good news and healing people everywhere.

7 Now Herod the tetrarch heard about all that was going on. And he was perplexed because some were saying that John had been raised from the dead, 8 others that Elijah had appeared, and still others that one of the prophets of long ago had come back to life. 9 But Herod said, "I beheaded John. Who, then, is this I hear such things about?" And he tried to see him.

## Jesus Feeds the Five Thousand

10 When the apostles returned, they reported to Jesus what they had done. Then he took them with him and they withdrew by themselves to a town called Bethsaida, 11 but the crowds learned about it and followed him. He welcomed them and spoke to them about the kingdom of God, and healed those who needed healing.

12 Late in the afternoon the Twelve came to him and said, "Send the crowd away so they can go to the surrounding villages and countryside and find food and lodging, because we are in a remote place here."

13 He replied, "You give them something to eat."

They answered, "We have only five loaves of bread and two fish—unless we go and buy food for all this crowd." 14 (About five thousand men were there.)

But he said to his disciples, "Have them sit down in groups of about fifty each." 15 The disciples did so, and everyone sat down. 16 Taking the five loaves and the two fish and looking up to heaven, he gave thanks and broke them. Then he gave them to the disciples to distribute to the people. 17 They all ate and were satisfied, and the disciples picked up twelve baskets of broken pieces that were left over.

## Peter Declares That Jesus Is the Messiah

18 Once when Jesus was praying in private and his disciples were with him, he asked them, "Who do the crowds say I am?"

19 They replied, "Some say John the Baptist; others say Elijah; and still others, that one of the prophets of long ago has come back to life."

20 "But what about you?" he asked. "Who do you say I am?"

Peter answered, "God's Messiah."

## Jesus Predicts His Death

21 Jesus strictly warned them not to tell this to anyone. 22 And he said, "The Son of Man must suffer many things and be rejected by the elders, the chief priests and the teachers of the law, and he must be killed and on the third day be raised to life."

23 Then he said to them all: "Whoever wants to be my disciple must deny themselves and take up their cross daily and follow me. 24 For whoever wants to save their life will lose it, but whoever loses their life for me will save it. 25 What good is it for someone to gain the whole world, and yet lose or forfeit their very self? 26 Whoever is ashamed of me and my words, the Son of Man will be ashamed of them when he comes in his glory and in the glory of the Father and of the holy angels.

27 "Truly I tell you, some who are standing here will not taste death before they see the kingdom of God."

## The Transfiguration

28 About eight days after Jesus said this, he took Peter, John and James with him and went up onto a mountain to pray. 29 As he was praying, the appearance of his face changed, and his clothes became as bright as a flash of lightning. 30 Two men, Moses and Elijah, appeared in glorious splendor, talking with Jesus. 31 They spoke about his departure,[a] which he was about to bring to fulfillment at Jerusalem. 32 Peter and his companions were very sleepy, but when they became fully awake, they saw his glory and the two men standing with him. 33 As the men were leaving Jesus, Peter said to him, "Master, it is good for us to be here. Let us put up three shelters—one for you, one for Moses and one for Elijah." (He did not know what he was saying.)

34 While he was speaking, a cloud appeared and covered them, and they were afraid as they entered the cloud. 35 A voice came from the cloud, saying, "This is my Son, whom I have chosen; listen to him." 36 When the voice had spoken, they found that Jesus was alone. The disciples kept this to themselves and did not tell anyone at that time what they had seen.

## Jesus Heals a Demon-Possessed Boy

37 The next day, when they came down from the mountain, a large crowd met him. 38 A man in the crowd called out, "Teacher, I beg you to look at my son, for he is my only child. 39 A spirit seizes him and he suddenly screams; it throws him into convulsions so that he foams at the mouth. It scarcely ever leaves him and is destroying him. 40 I begged your disciples to drive it out, but they could not."

41 "You unbelieving and perverse generation," Jesus replied, "how long shall I stay with you and put up with you? Bring your son here."

42 Even while the boy was coming, the demon threw him to the ground in a convulsion. But Jesus rebuked the impure spirit, healed the boy

and gave him back to his father. 43 And they were all amazed at the greatness of God.

## Jesus Predicts His Death a Second Time

While everyone was marveling at all that Jesus did, he said to his disciples, 44 "Listen carefully to what I am about to tell you: The Son of Man is going to be delivered into the hands of men." 45 But they did not understand what this meant. It was hidden from them, so that they did not grasp it, and they were afraid to ask him about it.

46 An argument started among the disciples as to which of them would be the greatest. 47 Jesus, knowing their thoughts, took a little child and had him stand beside him. 48 Then he said to them, "Whoever welcomes this little child in my name welcomes me; and whoever welcomes me welcomes the one who sent me. For it is the one who is least among you all who is the greatest."

# Luke 9 Reflection

## Who Is the Greatest?

This is an extraordinary chapter!

Jesus fed 5,000 people with only a couple loaves of bread and a few fish. The disciples got to be a part of this stunning miracle as they handed out food and wound up with 12 baskets full of leftovers!

Jesus took Peter, James and John up on a mountain to pray. The text says Jesus' appearance changed. Moses and Elijah show up! The Transfiguration happens, and the disciples are right there in the middle of it!

A man with a demon-possessed son approached and asked Jesus to heal his boy. He said he asked the disciples to do it. They could not. Jesus healed the boy, and everyone was amazed at the greatness of God. The bible says while everyone was still processing the healing of the possessed boy, Jesus turned to His disciples and predicted His death. But they couldn't understand what He was saying. It went right over their heads.

As they were still standing there, the disciples started arguing about who is the greatest among them. Are you kidding me? How unaware are these guys? How self-absorbed must they have been? Read the room, bro! They were the ones who passed out the food to the 5,000. They literally watched as the food expanded knowing they had nothing to do with it. They were there, shaking in their sandals, as Jesus casually had a chat with Moses and Elijah. Who, by the way, had both been gone from the earth for about a thousand years.

Now they are standing in the middle of the crowd who are still shocked because Jesus had delivered the demon-possessed boy whom the disciples could not, and they are arguing among themselves over which one of them is going to be the greatest.

These poor, uneducated and unqualified fishermen have been chosen by Jesus to be a part of history changing, world altering events, and all they can do in that moment is focus on themselves.

Man! What knuckleheads. As I read the chapter I could feel my blood pressure rising.

But Jesus handles them with grace.
He doesn't demean them.
He doesn't punish them.

He simply speaks the truth about humility and servanthood.

In the middle of my judgmental attitude toward the disciples, I was reminded of the times throughout my life and ministry when Jesus was doing extraordinary things around me. Even miracles having nothing to do with me or my abilities. Yet He graciously allowed me to be a part of them. And my response was as selfish, prideful and arrogant as the disciples.

And as He responded to them,
He didn't demean me either.
He didn't punish me.
He simply spoke the truth to me.
He spoke truth about my identity in
Him, and He restored me as a son.

Jesus is so good.

# My Prayer

*Father,*

*On days when I am living from my humanity rather than from the Spirit, remind me again of humility and of servanthood. Remind me I am complete in You and there is nothing left to prove. Remind me I can relax and let You be the mediator. I can let you be my defender. I can let You be my provider.*

*Amen*

## What is the Spirit saying to You?

Your Reflection

___________________________________________

___________________________________________

___________________________________________

___________________________________________

Your Prayer

___________________________________________

___________________________________________

___________________________________________

___________________________________________

Today I will _______________________________

# luke 10

## Jesus Sends Out the Seventy-Two

1 After this the Lord appointed seventy-two[a] others and sent them two by two ahead of him to every town and place where he was about to go. 2 He told them, "The harvest is plentiful, but the workers are few. Ask the Lord of the harvest, therefore, to send out workers into his harvest field. 3 Go! I am sending you out like lambs among wolves. 4 Do not take a purse or bag or sandals; and do not greet anyone on the road.

5 "When you enter a house, first say, 'Peace to this house.' 6 If someone who promotes peace is there, your peace will rest on them; if not, it will return to you. 7 Stay there, eating and drinking whatever they give you, for the worker deserves his wages. Do not move around from house to house.

8 "When you enter a town and are welcomed, eat what is offered to you. 9 Heal the sick who are there and tell them, 'The kingdom of God has come near to you.' 10 But when you enter a town and are not welcomed, go into its streets and say, 11 'Even the dust of your town we wipe from our feet as a warning to you. Yet be sure of this: The kingdom of God has come near.' 12 I tell you, it will be more bearable on that day for Sodom than for that town.

# Luke 10 Reflection

## The Spirit Knows

Jesus sends his disciples out and tells them if they go into a town and are not accepted, to wipe the dust off their feet and say to them it will be better for Sodom than for them.

Jesus also tells us in other places to contend in prayer. He says, ask and keep asking. Seek and keep seeking. Knock and keep knocking.

What do you do when Jesus says to do two different things? Do we contend or do we wipe the dust off our feet and keep it moving?

I think the answer is yes and yes.

How do we know the difference? We don't. Our feelings or our thoughts get in the way. We are clouded by our own experiences and memories. Our trigger points and trauma inform us much more quickly than we care to admit. Given those realities, how are we supposed to know when to contend and when to move along?

I believe we have to do two things. First, we have to listen to the voice of the Holy Spirit. Here's the hard part. Then we have to obey what we heard the Spirit say.

He speaks to us all. He speaks through His Word. He speaks through other people. He speaks through circumstances. He reminds us of the things Jesus said. He speaks to some through dreams and visions. He speaks to others through imagery. Some people sense certain things around them. Some people have a feeling or a knowing.

I am a "knower."

There's a certain confidence that comes when the Spirit is saying something to me. It's not a question of logic or convenience. It's a matter of peace and confidence in what needs to happen or be accomplished.

Have you ever been faced with a decision where, if it were up to you, the choice would be easy?

But there's a nagging little thing inside of you that kind of knows you are supposed to do the thing you don't want to do?

Sometimes it means you have to suck up some pride and be kind to someone who has hurt you. Sometimes it means you have to stay at a job you would rather leave. Sometimes it means leaving when you would rather stay. When He is saying things I don't necessarily want to hear are the moments I am the most confident, it is Him.

I remember a time when Gwen and I were given an opportunity to serve at a church where we had previously been hurt. Nothing in either of us really wanted to go. We were honest about our misgivings. The Pastor was gracious and understood the feelings. He asked us to pray.

So we prayed for clarity. OK. I'll be honest. I prayed God would say, "No." Except He didn't.

In the end, against our own human judgment and preference, we were obedient to His voice and made the move and served. It was not an easy thing to do. And, if I'm honest, I kind of moved into it in an emotional karate stance. But we did it. We could not have ever seen it coming, nor would I have predicted it, but some of those whose words caused the wounds became the very ones who helped us heal.

God knows these things and has a way of speaking to us through the Holy Spirit. That's His part. He speaks. We listen and obey. That's our part.

It has to be what Peter was feeling when they had been fishing all night and caught nothing. Jesus shows up in the morning and gives the sim-

　　　LISTENING THROUGH LUKE

plistic, even naive, instruction to 'drop your net on the other side of the boat.' Peter must have thought, "Seriously? The other side of the boat?" They had undoubtedly thrown their nets on both sides of the boat, over and over, all night long.

Peter is a professional. Yes, he is prideful and impetuous but he knows how to fish!

My intuition tells me Peter wanted to not throw the nets on the other side of the boat. It must have taken all he had to muster up a smidgen of humility and speak the words with as little sarcasm as possible.

Try to imagine the scene:

"Lord …. We've been fishing all night! … (long dramatic pause) …

But because You say so … (silent eye roll) …..

We will throw our nets on the other side of the boat."

The very next moment, they caught such a load of fish they needed help to haul them all in. If Peter had not listened and obeyed, he would have missed it. If my wife and I had not pressed through our thoughts and feelings and said, "yes" to His call, we would likely have missed a fair amount of blessing as well.

How do we know when it is the right time to contend or to wipe the dust off of our feet and move along? We often don't. But the Holy Spirit knows. We just have to know what the voice of the Holy Spirit sounds like and then be obedient to it.

# My Prayer

*Father,*

*Give me ears to hear and a heart to obey. Even in the moments, especially in the moments when my flesh wants to do the opposite. Give me faith enough to swallow my pride and see past my experience and simply be obedient to the voice of the Holy Spirit.*

*Amen*

**What is the Spirit saying to You?**

Your Reflection

________________________________________

________________________________________

________________________________________

________________________________________

Your Prayer

________________________________________

________________________________________

________________________________________

Today I will __________________________________

# luke 11

## Jesus' Teaching on Prayer

1 One day Jesus was praying in a certain place. When he finished, one of his disciples said to him, "Lord, teach us to pray, just as John taught his disciples."

2 He said to them, "When you pray, say:

> "'Father,[a]
> hallowed be your name,
> your kingdom come.[b]
> 3 Give us each day our daily bread.
> 4 Forgive us our sins,
> for we also forgive everyone who sins against us.[c]
> And lead us not into temptation.[d]'"

5 Then Jesus said to them, "Suppose you have a friend, and you go to him at midnight and say, 'Friend, lend me three loaves of bread; 6 a friend of mine on a journey has come to me, and I have no food to offer him.' 7 And suppose the one inside answers, 'Don't bother me. The door is already locked, and my children and I are in bed. I can't get up and give you anything.' 8 I tell you, even though he will not get up and give you the bread because of friendship, yet because of your shameless audacity[e] he will surely get up and give you as much as you need.

9 "So I say to you: Ask and it will be given to you; seek and you will find; knock and the door will be opened to you. 10 For everyone who asks receives; the one who seeks finds; and to the one who knocks, the door will be opened.

11 "Which of you fathers, if your son asks for[f] a fish, will give him a snake instead? 12 Or if he asks for an egg, will give him a scorpion? 13 If you then, though you are evil, know how to give good gifts to your children, how much more will your Father in heaven give the Holy Spirit to those who ask him!"

# Luke 11 Reflection

## Our Father

The chapter opens up with Jesus teaching the disciples how to pray. He begins with the opening line, "Our Father…"

The word 'Father' indicates a very personal relationship. It is translated as 'daddy' or 'papa'.

This is a radically different idea because the prayers of the day were not personal. They prayed to God as majestic and transcendent, which He is. But they certainly did not see Him as warm and approachable like a Father.

"Our Father." Jesus levels the playing field. He doesn't position himself as better or higher, even though He is.

"Our Father." says we are all God's children. Even Jesus was His son. His 'Only Begotten' son.

"Our Father." He didn't say 'My Father'. He is telling us we need one another. We are not meant to do life outside of a community.

He builds on the idea of community by praying:

"Give *us* this day our daily bread."
"Forgive *us* our trespasses."
"Lead *us* not into temptation"
"Deliver *us* from evil."

We are all in this together. We need each other. We have a God who is our Father. He is good, and He cares.

He then tells a story about a man going to his friend's house because he needs some bread for a surprise guest. The man is already in bed. The kids are already sleeping, but because they are friends, the man gets up and gets his friend what he needs. Jesus is not only saying God is our Father, who is available and approachable. But He is bringing into focus that God is also our friend.

Jesus says, Ask and it will be given to you; Seek, and you will find; Knock, and the door will be opened to you. Ask, seek, knock. These are present tense imperative words in the Greek language. It's the same as saying, "Ask and keep on asking. Seek and keep on seeking. Knock and keep on knocking."

He asks them, "Which of you fathers, if your son asks for a fish, will give him a snake instead? Or if he asks for an egg, will give him a scorpion? If you then, though you are evil, know how to give good gifts to your children, how much more will your Father in heaven give the Holy Spirit to those who ask him!"

In a culture that told them Father God is grand and majestic. Aloof and far off. Jesus says something different. Jesus says He is our Father and Friend. Friends get out of bed in the middle of the night to get their friends what they need. Fathers don't give their kids snakes when they ask for fish. Not even evil fathers do that.

When the Disciples asked how we should pray, He wanted them to know then, as He wants us to know now. Our whole life should be marked by a constant pursuit, and an ongoing posture of trust and dependence on Father God. Because He is good and He wants what is best for us. Always.

Some of us are not sure about that, though.

Maybe you want to see Him as good, but there is a hesitancy to fully embrace it. Maybe your personal experience with your earthly father may not have been entirely healthy or warm. It might be that your earthly father was absent. Maybe he was there but detached and silent, which can be harder to reconcile than an absent father. Maybe there were abuse issues either by deeds or words.

            LISTENING THROUGH LUKE

Whatever our history, we tend to see our Heavenly Father through the lens of our earthly father.

We don't necessarily think about it. It's not a choice we make. It's our default setting of how we view things. I believe it is how God designed it. Fathers are supposed to give their children a healthy mindset of what a father is. Fathers are supposed to be upright, noble and good. That was the plan.

But we live in a broken world. As a result, we were all raised by broken fathers who were raised by broken fathers. If there are any feelings of anger there, I get it. But if you are a father, consider this. Your children have a broken father too. And on and on it goes.

The truth is, we are all a mess. We are all broken into pieces. We have issues.

I have issues.

    You have issues.

        All God's children have issues.

Not all earthly fathers are intentionally bad or evil. Some of us try real hard to be Godly examples for our families. But we are broken, and we make mistakes. We let people we love down. We disappoint those we love the most. It's simply the reality.

My wife and I told our sons they will likely need therapy, and it will be because of something we did or said. We will try to minimize your need for it as much as we can, but there may come a time when you need to find a good Christian counselor, and you will need to talk about us. Please do it. Do not feel bad. Use our names. Get it out and allow the truth to be identified.

Here's the truth:

Father God is the only Father who has no issues.
He is the only Father who can be fully trusted.
He is the only Father who will never leave you or forsake you.
He is good and He wants what is best for us.

Always.

# My Prayer

*Father,*

*In the moments when I am worried or in some kind of distress or anxiety, remind me You are good. Remind me You are present. Remind me You have my best in mind and You are working all things together for my good.*

*Amen*

## What is the Spirit saying to You?

Your Reflection

_______________________________________________

_______________________________________________

_______________________________________________

_______________________________________________

Your Prayer

_______________________________________________

_______________________________________________

_______________________________________________

_______________________________________________

Today I will _______________________________________

# luke 12

## Do Not Worry

22 Then Jesus said to his disciples: "Therefore I tell you, do not worry about your life, what you will eat; or about your body, what you will wear. 23 For life is more than food, and the body more than clothes. 24 Consider the ravens: They do not sow or reap, they have no storeroom or barn; yet God feeds them. And how much more valuable you are than birds! 25 Who of you by worrying can add a single hour to your life[b]? 26 Since you cannot do this very little thing, why do you worry about the rest?

27 "Consider how the wild flowers grow. They do not labor or spin. Yet I tell you, not even Solomon in all his splendor was dressed like one of these. 28 If that is how God clothes the grass of the field, which is here today, and tomorrow is thrown into the fire, how much more will he clothe you—you of little faith! 29 And do not set your heart on what you will eat or drink; do not worry about it. 30 For the pagan world runs after all such things, and your Father knows that you need them. 31 But seek his kingdom, and these things will be given to you as well.

32 "Do not be afraid, little flock, for your Father has been pleased to give you the kingdom. 33 Sell your possessions and give to the poor. Provide purses for yourselves that will not wear out, a treasure in heaven that will never fail, where no thief comes near and no moth destroys. 34 For where your treasure is, there your heart will be also.

# Luke 12 Reflection

## Don't Worry

Two very simple words which have been a challenge for me most of my life. I can get in my head. I can overthink. It is not my life motto, but I have heard it said, "Why pray when I can worry?" I like predictability. I am not a fan of quick change. I am a creature of habit. I don't like surprises. I don't like being pressured in that way.

My wife, Gwen, had a dream long ago. She is a prophetically gifted person who has had spiritual dreams throughout our married life. The Spirit tells her important things in her dreams. This particular dream had a bunch of our friends involved. We were all hanging out at a pool party, and Jesus was there with us. White robe, sash and all of it. We were all doing what people do at pool parties. Eating, talking, sunning and laughing. Enjoying the time with each other. At one point, Jesus got up and started making His way around the pool picking people up and throwing people into the water! She said people were having a blast, and Jesus was laughing along with all the rest. She said, in the dream, I was standing by the pool's edge with my back facing Jesus, which obviously made me an easy target for Him. He quietly walked to where I was. When He arrived where I was, He stopped. He let me know He was there and said something to me. We both smiled. He walked away and went on to throw someone else in the water.

As Gwen was unpacking the story, she remembered becoming mad at Jesus. Why would He push everyone else in the water except Mark? So, in the dream, dripping wet from recently being tossed into the pool, Gwen confronted Jesus, "Hey! Why didn't you throw Mark in the pool? You threw the rest of us in?"

She said, "Jesus turned and looked at me with those peaceful eyes and said, 'Mark doesn't like to be pushed.' "

There are some things that only Jesus can say to your spouse.

The truth is, I don't like to be pushed. I don't like being put on the spot. I like knowing what's around the corner, and I like being a part of the decision-making process if what's around the corner is going to change. That's not a bad thing. God wired me that way for a reason and a purpose. I am an arranger. I like things in their place.

However, following Jesus brings with it a steady stream of unpredictability. It offers a glorious lack of comfort zones. Life in Him can be an exercise in stretching. He knows that. He has to know that! Yet, He says, "Don't worry."

For me, most days, not worrying is easier said than done. Yet my mind knows we were never told to do something in scripture we are not equipped to do. The Bible never says to go to the top of tall buildings and flap your arms and fly safely to the ground. We are not equipped to fly, so we are never told to do so. However, we are told to not worry. Because we can. Because we are equipped with the capacity to do so.

My flesh battles with it, but my heart longs for the spontaneous joy of His presence.

# My Prayer

*Father,*

*Help me to balance the pressing needs of the day with the reality and promises of eternity. Help me to relax and trust You with it all. Help me to balance the way You have wired me with the necessity to let go and simply follow You. Help me to trust You know where I am and You know what I need. Help me to not worry. Even if that means getting tossed into the pool from time to time, even though You know I don't like it.*

*Amen*

## What is the Spirit saying to You?

Your Reflection

_______________________________________

_______________________________________

_______________________________________

_______________________________________

Your Prayer

_______________________________________

_______________________________________

_______________________________________

_______________________________________

Today I will _______________________________

luke 13

## Jesus Heals a Crippled Woman on the Sabbath

10 On a Sabbath Jesus was teaching in one of the synagogues, 11 and a woman was there who had been crippled by a spirit for eighteen years. She was bent over and could not straighten up at all. 12 When Jesus saw her, he called her forward and said to her, "Woman, you are set free from your infirmity." 13 Then he put his hands on her, and immediately she straightened up and praised God.

14 Indignant because Jesus had healed on the Sabbath, the synagogue leader said to the people, "There are six days for work. So come and be healed on those days, not on the Sabbath."

15 The Lord answered him, "You hypocrites! Doesn't each of you on the Sabbath untie your ox or donkey from the stall and lead it out to give it water? 16 Then should not this woman, a daughter of Abraham, whom Satan has kept bound for eighteen long years, be set free on the Sabbath day from what bound her?"

17 When he said this, all his opponents were humiliated, but the people were delighted with all the wonderful things he was doing.

The Parables of the Mustard Seed and the Yeast

18 Then Jesus asked, "What is the kingdom of God like? What shall I compare it to? 19 It is like a mustard seed, which a man took and planted in his garden. It grew and became a tree, and the birds perched in its branches."

20 Again he asked, "What shall I compare the kingdom of God to? 21 It is like yeast that a woman took and mixed into about sixty pounds[a] of flour until it worked all through the dough."

## The Narrow Door

22 Then Jesus went through the towns and villages, teaching as he made his way to Jerusalem. 23 Someone asked him, "Lord, are only a few people going to be saved?"

He said to them, 24 "Make every effort to enter through the narrow door, because many, I tell you, will try to enter and will not be able to.

# Luke 13 Reflection

## Faith or Works?

Jesus chastises some Pharisees for being upset he healed a woman on the sabbath which is a clear violation of the Law. The Law represents a "works"-based religion. Legalism. Legalism demands you earn your way to salvation, which is simply not possible.

Jesus introduces the idea of Grace as He says to the Pharisees, "Even you guys untie your ox or donkey on the sabbath and lead them to water to drink. This woman, who is a daughter of Abraham, has been tied up for years! Isn't it great that she, too, can be unbound on the sabbath as well?" (paraphrased, of course) It is quite a moment. The Scriptures say the Pharisees were humiliated at their obvious hypocrisy.

The life of faith is not about keeping the rules and regulations. It's about Grace.

Grace is about relationship.
Grace is about resting in the fact Jesus did all that was necessary.
Grace is about knowing we don't have to perform or measure up.

But just a few verses later, Jesus is talking about the "Narrow Door." He says, "Only a few find it." He says, "Do all you can to enter the narrow door." Some versions say 'work hard to enter.'

So what is it? Are we saved by grace through faith, or are we to work hard to enter? Just like a previous reflection, I believe the answer is, once again, yes and yes.

For some context, I used to struggle with flesh issues. Nothing uncommon to most men. The pornography industry banks on the fact men are visually stimulated. We are and I had fallen prey. Try as I might in my own power, I couldn't seem to detach myself from its grip and felt powerless to defeat it on my own.

I would pray the Holy Spirit would magically take things away because I know God can heal instantaneously. I personally know of miraculous stories of addictions being gone in an instant, and the person never fighting against it after that moment. God can do it. It is my experience, however, most of the time the Holy Spirit is looking for a partnership with us.

I have heard well-meaning people say all we need is a touch from the Holy Spirit and our lives will be radically different. I don't disagree. I have watched the Holy Spirit absolutely free a bound person. However, if after a freeing touch of the Holy Spirit, we go back to bad and destructive habits, we can negate whatever it is the Holy Spirit is trying to do in us.

Partnership.

Years ago, I was overweight by about 50 lbs. I couldn't tie my shoes without losing my breath. I was breaking out in hives every time I would eat. Something had to change. I decided to do a 40-day fast with juices only. I got a vegetable juicer. I was determined to change my physical body to a healthier version of myself.

And you know what? After getting in the right state of mind, along with the love and support of my family and the empowerment of the Holy Spirit, I did it! 40 days with no food! Are you kidding me? I lost 40 pounds in those 40 days! People noticed the difference. They would ask me how I felt during the fast. My reply would be, "HUNGRY!! How do you think I felt? I wasn't eating FOOOOOOD!!"

My life changed! I could move more easily. Exercise was not as painful. I developed definition in my abdominal muscles. Something my wife liked very much! I began running and worked my way up to half-marathon distances. All of this happened in my mid to late 40's. It was incredible!

At some point after the fast, the reality set in. I had just said 'no' to food for 40 days. Something pretty critical to a human's existence. If my spirit man could tell my flesh man, "No" to food, how many far less critical

   LISTENING THROUGH LUKE

things had I allowed to rule my life? In how many other ways had I allowed my flesh man to tell my spirit man, the way things were going to work?

I learned it is my spirit man who must inform my flesh man. Not the other way around. But it has to be intentional. It has to be a choice of which 'man' I will listen to.

The spirit or the flesh.

I have heard when some people fast, they have visions and dream dreams. Some people get super deep revelations from the Throne Room of God. That didn't happen for me. I mostly just stayed hungry. Why do they call it fasting anyway? It feels like it goes so slow.

I came out of that time empowered by the knowledge and experience, that if the Holy Spirit calls me to something, He will also give me the strength to accomplish it and see it through.

Partnership.

Grace is not a license for a lazy faith life. Becoming like Jesus does not happen accidentally.
We must pursue Him and His righteousness.
We must put away childish things.
We must take up our cross and follow Him.
We are saved by grace through faith alone.

We must also 'do all we can to enter.'

# My Prayer

*Father,*

*In the tension of my day, allow me to find the balance of grace and partnership. Help me to embrace your amazing Grace as the gift that it is. May it be my motivation to partner with You BECAUSE of Grace and not as a way to EARN it.*

*Amen*

## What is the Spirit saying to You?

Your Reflection

_______________________________________

_______________________________________

_______________________________________

_______________________________________

Your Prayer

_______________________________________

_______________________________________

_______________________________________

_______________________________________

Today I will _______________________________

luke 14

## Jesus at a Pharisee's House

1 One Sabbath, when Jesus went to eat in the house of a prominent
Pharisee, he was being carefully watched. 2 There in front of him was
a man suffering from abnormal swelling of his body. 3 Jesus asked the
Pharisees and experts in the law, "Is it lawful to heal on the Sabbath or
not?" 4 But they remained silent. So taking hold of the man, he healed
him and sent him on his way.

5 Then he asked them, "If one of you has a child[a] or an ox that falls
into a well on the Sabbath day, will you not immediately pull it out?" 6
And they had nothing to say.

7 When he noticed how the guests picked the places of honor at the
table, he told them this parable: 8 "When someone invites you to a
wedding feast, do not take the place of honor, for a person more dis-
tinguished than you may have been invited. 9 If so, the host who invited
both of you will come and say to you, 'Give this person your seat.' Then,
humiliated, you will have to take the least important place. 10 But when
you are invited, take the lowest place, so that when your host comes,
he will say to you, 'Friend, move up to a better place.' Then you will be
honored in the presence of all the other guests. 11 For all those who
exalt themselves will be humbled, and those who humble themselves
will be exalted."

12 Then Jesus said to his host, "When you give a luncheon or dinner,
do not invite your friends, your brothers or sisters, your relatives, or your
rich neighbors; if you do, they may invite you back and so you will be
repaid. 13 But when you give a banquet, invite the poor, the crippled,
the lame, the blind, 14 and you will be blessed. Although they cannot
repay you, you will be repaid at the resurrection of the righteous."

# Luke 14 Reflection

## Humility - The Seat of Honor

All through this chapter, Jesus is trying to move people toward humility.

Don't take the seats of honor. Sit in the lowest places. Let the host take you to the good seats.

When you throw a banquet, don't throw a party to be noticed with the intent to then get invited to other people's parties. Invite people who cannot repay you. Invite the crippled, the lame, the blind, the poor. He says, "to follow me, you have to lay it all down."

It is at the heart of who Jesus is. After all, He left his throne in heaven and humbled Himself to come live as one of us. He says those who exalt themselves will be humbled, and those who humble themselves will be exalted.

Humility.

I have written this before, and I will likely write it again. I used to struggle with my worth and my value. That struggle quietly led to my trying to earn approval. Trying to get things right so I would be valued and validated. I had preached about Identity in Christ for years, yet I had never allowed that truth to move from my head down into my heart. I believed a lie, buried deep in my soul, that I somehow had to earn that place and that position in Him.

I quietly worked for His approval. I worked to be good enough. I never set out with that goal in mind, but I absolutely behaved and worked as though somewhere in my human condition, I could measure up on my own merit. The lie said somehow, I could do enough good stuff for Him to notice me and approve of me.

Without realizing it, I was trying to seat myself in the Place of Honor Jesus talks about in this passage. It subtly disguised itself as sacrificial service for the Lord and the Kingdom. It looked awfully noble and humble to those around me and those I served. It wasn't humility. It was pride.

How could it be pride? I gave my life to ministry. I gave my heart to the kingdom. I sacrificed time away from my wife and kids to the detriment of our family's health and my marriage. I did it all for the betterment of the people in my care.

Pride?

Yes, because I was doing it to be noticed and earn something.

Approval
      Validation
            Acceptance

It was pride because I was working to be good enough rather than resting on the Grace Jesus died to give me.

I can take you to the very spot where everything changed for me.

Gwen and I were in crisis because trying to minister for the reward of affirmation and validation will suck the life out of you. I had pulled out of full-time vocational ministry because we were free-falling. We needed a break. We needed to be healed. We were hurting and I was reeling. If I was not Pastor Mark, then who was I going to be? My entire identity and sense of value and worth was wrapped up in that title.

I remember going down for prayer at the church we attended at the time. While I was standing there waiting for prayer, a friend of mine on the prayer team approached me. He did not know what was happening in our lives, nor did he ask. He began speaking over me in one of the most affirming prophetic ways I have ever been spoken to. It was like Jesus Himself was standing in front of me, telling me who I was. Telling me I was OK. Telling me He liked me. Telling me He didn't need anything from me to love me.

I have no other way to describe what happened to me except in that moment, the reality of who I am in Christ moved out of my head into my heart. Truth was spoken. Lies were revealed. As the reality of my Sonship suddenly came alive in my soul, I became a sobbing mess on the floor at the feet of my buddy, who had no idea what he had just done.

My life has been different from that very moment. My Sonship in Christ is complete, and the work is finished. The work was done by Jesus; therefore, it is not based on me. It literally has nothing to do with me. Living in that reality allows me to sit at the lowest seat at the table and be completely confident and comfortable knowing I am His.

I have no need to impress or to strive.

    Because I am seen.

      I am known.

        I am enough.

# My Prayer

*Father,*

*Thank you for sending Jesus to pay the price I could never pay. Thank you for doing the work I could never do. Thank you for calling me your Son without needing me to perform or measure up to earn it. Your grace is amazing.*

*Amen*

**What is the Spirit saying to You?**

Your Reflection

______________________________________________

______________________________________________

______________________________________________

______________________________________________

Your Prayer

______________________________________________

______________________________________________

______________________________________________

______________________________________________

Today I will ______________________________________

# luke 15

## The Parable of the Lost Sheep

1 Now the tax collectors and sinners were all gathering around to hear Jesus. 2 But the Pharisees and the teachers of the law muttered, "This man welcomes sinners and eats with them."

3 Then Jesus told them this parable: 4 "Suppose one of you has a hundred sheep and loses one of them. Doesn't he leave the ninety-nine in the open country and go after the lost sheep until he finds it? 5 And when he finds it, he joyfully puts it on his shoulders 6 and goes home. Then he calls his friends and neighbors together and says, 'Rejoice with me; I have found my lost sheep.' 7 I tell you that in the same way there will be more rejoicing in heaven over one sinner who repents than over ninety-nine righteous persons who do not need to repent.

## The Parable of the Lost Coin

8 "Or suppose a woman has ten silver coins[a] and loses one. Doesn't she light a lamp, sweep the house and search carefully until she finds it? 9 And when she finds it, she calls her friends and neighbors together and says, 'Rejoice with me; I have found my lost coin.' 10 In the same way, I tell you, there is rejoicing in the presence of the angels of God over one sinner who repents."

## The Parable of the Lost Son

11 Jesus continued: "There was a man who had two sons. 12 The younger one said to his father, 'Father, give me my share of the estate.' So he divided his property between them.

13 "Not long after that, the younger son got together all he had, set off for a distant country and there squandered his wealth in wild living. 14 After he had spent everything, there was a severe famine in that whole country, and he began to be in need. 15 So he went and hired himself out to a citizen of that country, who sent him to his fields to feed pigs. 16 He longed to fill his stomach with the pods that the pigs were eating, but no one gave him anything.

17 "When he came to his senses, he said, 'How many of my father's hired servants have food to spare, and here I am starving to death! 18 I will set out and go back to my father and say to him: Father, I have sinned against heaven and against you. 19 I am no longer worthy to be called your son; make me like one of your hired servants.' 20 So he got up and went to his father.

"But while he was still a long way off, his father saw him and was filled with compassion for him; he ran to his son, threw his arms around him and kissed him.

21 "The son said to him, 'Father, I have sinned against heaven and against you. I am no longer worthy to be called your son.'

22 "But the father said to his servants, 'Quick! Bring the best robe and put it on him. Put a ring on his finger and sandals on his feet. 23 Bring the fattened calf and kill it. Let's have a feast and celebrate. 24 For this son of mine was dead and is alive again; he was lost and is found.' So they began to celebrate.

25 "Meanwhile, the older son was in the field. When he came near the house, he heard music and dancing. 26 So he called one of the servants and asked him what was going on. 27 'Your brother has come,' he replied, 'and your father has killed the fattened calf because he has him back safe and sound.'

28 "The older brother became angry and refused to go in. So his father went out and pleaded with him. 29 But he answered his father, 'Look! All these years I've been slaving for you and never disobeyed your orders. Yet you never gave me even a young goat so I could celebrate with my friends. 30 But when this son of yours who has squandered your property with prostitutes comes home, you kill the fattened calf for him!'

31 "'My son,' the father said, 'you are always with me, and everything I have is yours. 32 But we had to celebrate and be glad, because this brother of yours was dead and is alive again; he was lost and is found.'"

# Luke 15 Reflection

## Sinners and Questionable People

Jesus is accused of hanging out and eating with sinners and other questionable people.

Immediately following are three of the most well-known parables in the Bible.

1. The Lost Sheep, where Jesus leaves the 99 to go get the one.

2. The Parable of the Lost Coin, where the whole house is turned upside down just to find one lost coin.

3. Then, the famous Prodigal Son story.

All are awesome illustrations of God's pursuit of His children. In all honesty, I used to read the Prodigal Son story with some cynicism. Mainly, how does a guy in a pig pit suddenly and miraculously 'come to his senses'?

Some versions say, He 'came to himself.'

I mean, c'mon! It sounds a little like a jailhouse confession. How can a guy be living the life, doing his thing, all of a sudden 'wake up' and realize he needs to go back to his Father's House? Was it the money? If he still had money, would he not have continued as before?

Those were the questions I used to wonder about until ...

Until I had one of those moments where I, suddenly and miraculously came to myself. I will never forget it.

Paul writes in Ephesians to 'give no place to the devil'. The word 'place' is topos. It's where we get our word topography. It's used in map-making. It has to do with boundaries and borders. Paul is saying we can give the enemy areas in our lives from which to work. A foothold. A beachhead. A place to post up and fire lies and accusations. I had given 'place' to him, and my marriage and family was suffering because of it.

I will never forget sitting in our much-loved and trusted counselor's office. In one moment, I was justifying ridiculous behavior. Then in the next moment I could not only see how destructive my choices had been, but I could literally feel the weight of the pain and anxiety my choices had caused in my wife.

Coming to yourself is quite surreal and unexplainable.

At the time, I explained it as a cloud leaving my brain. The immediate internal reaction was, "Who has been making these decisions for me while I was asleep?" I used to try to describe it as clarity coming to me. The more I have thought and prayed about what happened that day, I now believe as our counselor spoke truth to me in her office, a spirit of deception I had given 'place' to simply had to go. Because deception cannot coexist with Truth.

I came to myself.

     I came to my senses.

          A spirit of deception left.

However you want to filter that, I was 'awake'. I was awake, alive and began running back to my wife. Back to my kids. Back to my Father's House.

I no longer question the validity of the Prodigal Son's miraculous turn around. I am forever grateful Jesus still hangs out and eats with questionable people.

Because I was one.

Thank you, Jesus. You are a great Savior, friend, and awesome brother.

# My Prayer

*Father,*

*Allow me to see others the way You see me. Just as You see me as a Son who is worthwhile enough to believe in, give me grace for others when they are struggling to understand who You are and how You love them. Thank you for believing in me when I did not believe in myself.*

*Amen*

## What is the Spirit saying to You?

Your Reflection

____________________________________________________

____________________________________________________

____________________________________________________

____________________________________________________

Your Prayer

____________________________________________________

____________________________________________________

____________________________________________________

____________________________________________________

Today I will ___________________________________________

luke 16

# The Parable of the Shrewd Manager

1 Jesus told his disciples: "There was a rich man whose manager was accused of wasting his possessions. 2 So he called him in and asked him, 'What is this I hear about you? Give an account of your management, because you cannot be manager any longer.'

3 "The manager said to himself, 'What shall I do now? My master is taking away my job. I'm not strong enough to dig, and I'm ashamed to beg— 4 I know what I'll do so that, when I lose my job here, people will welcome me into their houses.'

5 "So he called in each one of his master's debtors. He asked the first, 'How much do you owe my master?'

6 "'Nine hundred gallons[a] of olive oil,' he replied.

"The manager told him, 'Take your bill, sit down quickly, and make it four hundred and fifty.'

7 "Then he asked the second, 'And how much do you owe?'

"'A thousand bushels[b] of wheat,' he replied.

"He told him, 'Take your bill and make it eight hundred.'

8 "The master commended the dishonest manager because he had acted shrewdly. For the people of this world are more shrewd in dealing with their own kind than are the people of the light. 9 I tell you, use worldly wealth to gain friends for yourselves, so that when it is gone, you will be welcomed into eternal dwellings.

10 "Whoever can be trusted with very little can also be trusted with much, and whoever is dishonest with very little will also be dishonest with much. 11 So if you have not been trustworthy in handling worldly wealth, who will trust you with true riches? 12 And if you have not been trustworthy with someone else's property, who will give you property of your own?

13 "No one can serve two masters. Either you will hate the one and love the other, or you will be devoted to the one and despise the other. You cannot serve both God and money."

14 The Pharisees, who loved money, heard all this and were sneering at Jesus. 15 He said to them, "You are the ones who justify yourselves in the eyes of others, but God knows your hearts. What people value highly is detestable in God's sight.

## God and Money

You can't serve both God and money.

You can't live a life of faith in God and live a life of faith in money and wealth. You have to pick one.

It's not that money is bad. It's that our tendency is to shift our faith toward it. We tend to shift our sense of security and even our value and worth over to money away from God. I would like to say no matter what is going on in my bank account I am perfectly content. I would like to say worry and anxiety never rear their ugly head.

But that would not be a true statement.

I don't like it when money is tight. It makes me nervous. Banks and creditors expect the money they have loaned me to be repaid in steady installments. They are not concerned with my faith life or my dependence upon Jesus to provide.

So, yea. I don't like it when money is thin.

It's not that I don't trust Him to provide. But I would feel much better if I knew how He was going to do it. It's also not that He hasn't provided miraculously already! Gwen and I have seen Him do crazy things for us financially. Not just once. We have seen Him do it over and over again!

Not to pile on, but when my wife and I said yes to ministry all those years ago, we understood what that meant. We understood we were not going to live a life of extravagance. We understood we would need to live a frugal lifestyle. And we did. The entire time the boys were growing up, we sacrificed. We chose for Gwen not to work so that we could raise our sons. We wanted to be the ones to instill our Christian values in them and not leave it to a well-meaning daycare worker. No slight to daycare workers. I'm sure there are Godly daycare workers out there.

We never got past a paycheck-to-paycheck life throughout our ministry years. God always provided. And I still didn't like it when money is lacking. It still makes me nervous.  Every time.

Not too long ago, my oldest son who is now a husband and father to the coolest little grand dude in the world, called me up needing some help with some things. It's humbling to ask your father for help when you want to be the one who makes sure your family has what they need.

I told him his mother and I would always be here to help in any way we possibly could. That is what family is for. Somewhere in the conversation, he began to become emotional, saying his wife and son deserved better than what he was able to give them on this particular day.

Apparently, he's built like I am. He doesn't much like it either.

I found myself asking him some questions.

> "Son, are you aware of the fact that when you were a kid, your mom and I lived on the financial edge and rarely had any extra money for anything?"

> "Are you aware we were what some people would call poor?"

> "God has been faithful to us in our finances, and we are in a good spot now, but do you remember those days?"

He said, "Dad, I don't remember my childhood like that, at all."

I replied, "That's right! Because you always had what you needed, and most of the time, much of what you even wanted! God knows where you are, son. He knows what you need. He understands your heart to provide, because you are made in His image and He is our provider.

It makes sense the desire to provide and protect is in you, too. Try to relax and trust Him in the process."

(Maybe I should bookmark this page and read it back to myself the next time I am feeling anxious about money!)

       LISTENING THROUGH LUKE

It is a fine line, isn't it? Living in the tension between being anxious about not having enough money and being arrogant about having too much. It's a fine line and a delicate balance.

Hard work and good stewardship is indeed Biblical.

Providing for our families is good and noble.

But somewhere along the line, if we aren't careful to remember to routinely confess God is our provider, the hourglass can get turned upside down, and we can find ourselves putting faith in our abilities and money rather than God.

# My Prayer

*Father,*

*Give me grace to see you are the provider of all things. Even when things are tight, give me the grace to understand, much like my son when he was a little boy, there is no need to worry. As painful as it is for me to confess it, I don't need to know how You will provide. Give me the grace to live freely in the reality You will provide and You already have in so many ways. On days when I am not feeling the pinch, remind me it is still You who is providing even if it is through the gifts and abilities you have given me.*

*Amen*

**What is the Spirit saying to You?**

Your Reflection

_______________________________________________

_______________________________________________

_______________________________________________

_______________________________________________

Your Prayer

_______________________________________________

_______________________________________________

_______________________________________________

_______________________________________________

Today I will _______________________________________

# luke 17

## Sin, Faith, Duty

1 Jesus said to his disciples: "Things that cause people to stumble are bound to come, but woe to anyone through whom they come. 2 It would be better for them to be thrown into the sea with a millstone tied around their neck than to cause one of these little ones to stumble. 3 So watch yourselves.

"If your brother or sister[a] sins against you, rebuke them; and if they repent, forgive them. 4 Even if they sin against you seven times in a day and seven times come back to you saying 'I repent,' you must forgive them."

5 The apostles said to the Lord, "Increase our faith!"

6 He replied, "If you have faith as small as a mustard seed, you can say to this mulberry tree, 'Be uprooted and planted in the sea,' and it will obey you.

7 "Suppose one of you has a servant plowing or looking after the sheep. Will he say to the servant when he comes in from the field, 'Come along now and sit down to eat'? 8 Won't he rather say, 'Prepare my supper, get yourself ready and wait on me while I eat and drink; after that you may eat and drink'? 9 Will he thank the servant because he did what he was told to do? 10 So you also, when you have done everything you were told to do, should say, 'We are unworthy servants; we have only done our duty.'"

## Forgiveness

"Even if that person wrongs you seven times a day and each time turns again and asks forgiveness, you must forgive."

I have a problem with this one. My ministry experience tells me I'm not alone. Why would Jesus tell people to forgive those who have wronged you? Even if they do it seven times a day? It's hard to understand why Jesus would say that unless you don't understand what forgiveness is.

It might be easier to start with what forgiveness is not.

Forgiveness is <u>not</u> saying what a person did is now "OK." Some things will never be OK.

Forgiveness is also <u>not</u> putting yourself back in harm's way if you have been mistreated or abused.

Forgiveness does <u>not</u> require you to stay in abusive or toxic relationships.

*Then what is forgiveness?*

We want justice when we have been hurt. We want wrong to be made right. After all, we are made in the image of God, and God is the ultimate Judge. So, it is in us to want the things He wants. He wants justice, and so do we. Forgiveness is simply choosing to trust God to bring justice to our pain. It is confessing He can handle bringing justice to those who have hurt us much more thoroughly than we can.

I choose to trust God.

        I choose to let go of the pain.

                I choose to live free of the toxicity of holding on
to the hurt.

                        I choose to give it forward to Jesus.

In doing so, we can then walk in freedom and healing. Even to the point of praying those who hurt us are blessed.

It's not easy. When we are hurt and have suffered trauma, it is hard to see beyond it. When we have been taken advantage of or someone we thought we could trust lies to us or lets us down, it seems natural we should have the right to defend ourselves and make sure the other person understands what they have done and the hurt they have caused. It makes logical sense, but that's what God wants us to give to Him.

When we don't forgive, we are in effect saying we don't trust Father God to bring about justice on our behalf. The message is we are better equipped to bring about justice than He is.

I assure you. We are not.

He wants us free. He wants us to trust Him. He wants us to forgive. I know it doesn't seem fair. It doesn't seem fair because it is not. But the Bible never says God is fair. If God were fair, we would all get what we all deserve, and Jesus would never have come to save us from what we had coming..

I, for one, am glad He is not fair!

Bible does say He is just! He is far more capable of bringing about true justice than I will ever be. As I said, it is easy to see it when you are not the one who needs to forgive. It's another thing to be the one who has been hurt.

My wife and I were the object of some false accusations. The accusations were public and hurtful. The accusations were also completely false and out of left field. Even though we knew the truth and those clos-est to us found the accusations ridiculous, it was still extremely hurtful.

As a man whose integrity is important to him, I was angry. I wanted to fire back and defend myself and say all the nasty things on the same public forum used to accuse us. But I didn't. I knew it would not help anything and only make matters worse. But I also didn't want to forgive. What the person did was not okay, and I certainly didn't want to imply otherwise. They didn't deserve it.

I wanted an apology. I wanted them to take responsibility for their ac-tions and grovel for a while. I wanted justice.

But the Spirit reminded me, "while we were still sinners, Christ died for us."

Christ died for me.
        I did not deserve it.
                In all honesty, I deserved the opposite,
                        Yet He suffered in my place.

# My Prayer

*Father,*

*Help me to die to myself and become a little bit more like you each day. Thank you for saving me when I did not deserve it. Help me to forgive others even when they don't deserve it.*

*Amen*

## What is the Spirit saying to You?

Your Reflection

_______________________________________________

_______________________________________________

_______________________________________________

_______________________________________________

Your Prayer

_______________________________________________

_______________________________________________

_______________________________________________

_______________________________________________

Today I will _______________________________________________

luke 18

## The Parable of the Pharisee and the Tax Collector

9 To some who were confident of their own righteousness and looked down on everyone else, Jesus told this parable: 10 "Two men went up to the temple to pray, one a Pharisee and the other a tax collector. 11 The Pharisee stood by himself and prayed: 'God, I thank you that I am not like other people—robbers, evildoers, adulterers—or even like this tax collector. 12 I fast twice a week and give a tenth of all I get.'

13 "But the tax collector stood at a distance. He would not even look up to heaven, but beat his breast and said, 'God, have mercy on me, a sinner.'

14 "I tell you that this man, rather than the other, went home justified before God. For all those who exalt themselves will be humbled, and those who humble themselves will be exalted."

## The Little Children and Jesus

15 People were also bringing babies to Jesus for him to place his hands on them. When the disciples saw this, they rebuked them. 16 But Jesus called the children to him and said, "Let the little children come to me, and do not hinder them, for the kingdom of God belongs to such as these. 17 Truly I tell you, anyone who will not receive the kingdom of God like a little child will never enter it."

## The Rich and the Kingdom of God

18 A certain ruler asked him, "Good teacher, what must I do to inherit eternal life?"

19 "Why do you call me good?" Jesus answered. "No one is good—except God alone. 20 You know the commandments: 'You shall not commit adultery, you shall not murder, you shall not steal, you shall not give false testimony, honor your father and mother.'[a]"

21 "All these I have kept since I was a boy," he said.

22 When Jesus heard this, he said to him, "You still lack one thing. Sell everything you have and give to the poor, and you will have treasure in heaven. Then come, follow me."

23 When he heard this, he became very sad, because he was very wealthy. 24 Jesus looked at him and said, "How hard it is for the rich to enter the kingdom of God! 25 Indeed, it is easier for a camel to go through the eye of a needle than for someone who is rich to enter the kingdom of God."

# Luke 18 Reflection

## The Danger of Self-Sufficiency

The Parables of the Pharisees praying at the temple and the Rich Young Ruler bookend the portion of Scripture where Jesus says, 'anyone who will not receive the kingdom of God like a child will never enter into it.'

There is a clear contrast being made here by Luke. Dependency on God vs Dependency on Self. The Pharisee and the Rich Young Ruler suffer from the same thing.

Self-sufficiency. It can be subtle and often masks itself as righteousness. It masquerades as child-like faith. On the outside, it can look similar to dependence on God. Spending time in prayer. Spending time in the Word. Being charitable. Serving in the local church. Perhaps even making ministry your vocation as I did. The question is not: Am I doing the right things? The question is: Am I serving God to earn His acceptance, or do I understand I am fully accepted by God as I am, therefore I live for Him and serve Him?

It's a subtle difference. I heard an old preacher describe the difference this way, "Dressing modestly won't make you Holy. But if you are Holy, you will dress modestly."

Two people can be doing the same thing.

One person is living in the law.
>    The other person is living in grace.

One is being fed life.
>    The other is being robbed of it.

One person is living life thankful for the Cross.
>    The other person is trying to make the Cross of no effect.

Paul spoke about this in Galatians 2:21 - if righteousness could be gained through the Law, then Christ died for nothing. In other words, if I am sufficient, then what do I need Jesus for?

Let that sink in. It's a scary thought. We don't intentionally choose it. I know I didn't. That is the trap I fell into. That was my mindset.

I'm hoping there is an honest reader who can identify with the struggle of wanting to live with the childlike faith Jesus talked about, yet being driven, somehow, to perform for the acceptance of God. Well, I'm not the first, and neither are you.

It's an age-old struggle, and it goes all the way back to the Garden. Adam and Eve were enjoying life in the Garden with God. Walking and talking in the cool of the day. Processing their day. I often wonder what their conversations might have been like.

God giggling - "So tell me what you were thinking when you came up with the name, Platypus?'

Adam, laughing in response and shrugging his shoulders - "I don't know! It just came to me! It popped into my head, and it came out of my mouth before I could stop it!"

God - "Well, it's perfect!"

Think of a life like that! Their only experiences of life were with Him. In fact, the Bible says God breathed life into Adam. This required face-to-face contact. Can you imagine coming to consciousness nose to nose with the Creator of the universe?

It reminds me of a child whose father is a world-famous actor or athlete. The entire world is impressed by him and wants to be like him and clamors to be close to him. But the child has no other frame of reference for who this man is except that of being his child. The famous man is simply "Daddy." He's the one who comes running when the child falls to say everything is okay. He's the one who cheers on the child as he awkwardly learns how to somersault. He's the one who tucks her in at night. He's "Daddy."

What an existence!

Adam and Eve had no other perspective of God than that of Father. But because of the fall, Adam and Eve were no longer allowed to live with God in the Garden. Man was separated from Father God for the first time. And it has been mankind's pursuit ever since that moment, to work, strive and try to be good enough to get back into "Daddy's House."

But we can't. I can't. Not on my own merit. Not in my own ability. I need Jesus every day. I need to be reminded of His grace. I need His unmerited favor to bridge the gap I am incapable of bridging on my own.

I have lived a fair amount of life and have come to grips with my brokenness and weaknesses.

I have watched as Father God has taken my weaknesses and made them points where He can show His strength. My wife and I regularly share our story to encourage others who are struggling. I count it a privilege to share my woundedness and points of failure with others because when I do, it gives others a safe place to share theirs as well. I believe our ministry has become what James was speaking of when he said, "Confess your sins with one another so you can be healed."

I don't mean we sit and catalog all of the bad things we have done. Rather, we get honest about how life has wounded us. We talk about trauma pieces which are buried deep and, if left unidentified and unexposed, give life to other points of sin. We have seen beautiful moments of grace and healing come by the power of the Holy Spirit.

Still, if I am not careful, I will pick up that old mindset. I will once again pick up the old idea that unless I do and say all the right things, Father God will not be pleased with me.

I need Jesus
    You need Jesus
        We need Jesus

# My Prayer

*Father,*

*Make me aware of Your presence. Remind me You require nothing of me except surrender. On the days when I want to pick up the old tools of Self Sufficiency, remind me I am loved fully and completely. Remind me through no effort of my own, the gap between me and You has been restored. Remind me because of what my big brother Jesus did, I can come back to the Garden. Back to "Daddy's House"*

*Amen*

**What is the Spirit saying to You?**

Your Reflection

_______________________________________________

_______________________________________________

_______________________________________________

_______________________________________________

Your Prayer

_______________________________________________

_______________________________________________

_______________________________________________

_______________________________________________

Today I will _______________________________________

luke 19

## Zacchaeus the Tax Collector

1 Jesus entered Jericho and was passing through. 2 A man was there by the name of Zacchaeus; he was a chief tax collector and was wealthy. 3 He wanted to see who Jesus was, but because he was short he could not see over the crowd. 4 So he ran ahead and climbed a sycamore-fig tree to see him, since Jesus was coming that way.

5 When Jesus reached the spot, he looked up and said to him, "Zacchaeus, come down immediately. I must stay at your house today." 6 So he came down at once and welcomed him gladly.

7 All the people saw this and began to mutter, "He has gone to be the guest of a sinner."

8 But Zacchaeus stood up and said to the Lord, "Look, Lord! Here and now I give half of my possessions to the poor, and if I have cheated anybody out of anything, I will pay back four times the amount."

9 Jesus said to him, "Today salvation has come to this house, because this man, too, is a son of Abraham. 10 For the Son of Man came to seek and to save the lost."

## Room For Stupid People

Another story about Jesus choosing to spend time with sinners. This time, Jesus is with the notorious tax collector, Zacchaeus.

Not much is said about the things they talked about. All we know is whatever they talked about led to Zacchaeus's salvation and repentance. We also know the people were displeased and were grumbling about it. Can you imagine that? What gets into people? Seriously?

The Lord of Lords is saving a soul who will repent and spend eternity with Jesus in heaven! That ought to be reason enough to celebrate. But that's not all! Zacheus is going to not only give back what he stole from the people. He will actually bless them and give them more than he ever took.

And the people are displeased and grumbling.

My initial response is, "stupid people!" Why would they be unhappy about a man being transformed by Jesus? On a more self-serving note, Zacchaeus is getting ready to repay what he stole from you! Why don't you all shut up about it and let Jesus do what Jesus does!! A blessing is coming!

To be fair, Zaccheus had taken advantage of his position as a tax collector. The scriptures are clear about Tax Collectors and how they were thought of by the Jews. A Tax Collector was a Jew who partnered with the Roman government for their own enrichment at the expense of their Jewish brothers and sisters. Zacchaeus was the Chief Tax Collector. No doubt he became wealthy on the backs of some of the people who were now watching this scene unfold. The Jews were not happy about Jesus treating him with kindness and giving him the honor of visiting his house. Zacchaeus was never kind to them, and he definitely had not earned the honor Jesus was giving him.

They were not thrilled about what Jesus was doing. I get it.

If I'm honest, I have to say I have been displeased and grumbled about the way Jesus went about things in my life too. If it were up to me, many things would not have happened the way they did. But if those things had not happened, my life would look very much different than the way it does now. My perspective would not be what it is. I would not have the capacity to simply appreciate my wife's kindness. I would likely take it for granted.

Come to think of it, would I have even met her had things not transpired the way they did?

And if not, I would have never had the blessing of our two sons and their wives and our little grand dude.

God has blessed me with the coolest position in the marketplace one could ever ask for. One I would have never even thought to script or had the forethought to create for myself.

I like where He has me. I am truly enjoying this season of life more than any other season of my life so far. He really has blessed me with the truest and purest of riches! I didn't earn them. He has given me more than I could have ever imagined on my own.

And I was displeased and grumbled about the process just like that crowd long ago.

I am glad Jesus has room for "stupid people" in this story. And my story.

     LISTENING THROUGH LUKE

# My Prayer

*Father,*

*Help me to trust you in all things without complaint. Help me to see the best in my circumstances. Help me to stay true to You no matter how I feel. Help me not to be like the Pharisees or the Grumbling People, but rather more like Zacchaeus, who simply accepted you and whose life was radically transformed.*

*Amen*

## What is the Spirit saying to You?

Your Reflection

_______________________________________________

_______________________________________________

_______________________________________________

_______________________________________________

Your Prayer

_______________________________________________

_______________________________________________

_______________________________________________

_______________________________________________

Today I will _______________________________________

# luke 20

## The Authority of Jesus Questioned

1 One day as Jesus was teaching the people in the temple courts and proclaiming the good news, the chief priests and the teachers of the law, together with the elders, came up to him.

2 "Tell us by what authority you are doing these things," they said. "Who gave you this authority?"

3 He replied, "I will also ask you a question. Tell me: 4 John's baptism—was it from heaven, or of human origin?"

5 They discussed it among themselves and said, "If we say, 'From heaven,' he will ask, 'Why didn't you believe him?' 6 But if we say, 'Of human origin,' all the people will stone us, because they are persuaded that John was a prophet."

7 So they answered, "We don't know where it was from."

8 Jesus said, "Neither will I tell you by what authority I am doing these things."

## The Parable of the Tenants

9 He went on to tell the people this parable: "A man planted a vineyard, rented it to some farmers and went away for a long time. 10 At harvest time he sent a servant to the tenants so they would give him some of the fruit of the vineyard. But the tenants beat him and sent him away empty-handed. 11 He sent another servant, but that one also they beat and treated shamefully and sent away empty-handed. 12 He sent still a third, and they wounded him and threw him out.

13 "Then the owner of the vineyard said, 'What shall I do? I will send my son, whom I love; perhaps they will respect him.'

14 "But when the tenants saw him, they talked the matter over. 'This is the heir,' they said. 'Let's kill him, and the inheritance will be ours.' 15 So they threw him out of the vineyard and killed him.

"What then will the owner of the vineyard do to them? 16 He will come and kill those tenants and give the vineyard to others."

When the people heard this, they said, "God forbid!"

17 Jesus looked directly at them and asked, "Then what is the meaning of that which is written:

"'The stone the builders rejected

   has become the cornerstone'[a]?

18 Everyone who falls on that stone will be broken to pieces; anyone on whom it falls will be crushed."

19 The teachers of the law and the chief priests looked for a way to arrest him immediately, because they knew he had spoken this parable against them. But they were afraid of the people.

## Right or Reconciled

Jesus is all but revealing who He is to the Pharisees, Sadducees and Teachers of the Law, and they don't see it. From our perspective, it's hard to see how they could possibly miss it. But the details of the Law and the minutiae of their teachings keep getting in their way.

I remember as a young pastor being very excited about the church and my role in it.

I dove headfirst into all it demanded, and I was happy to do so. I remember thinking to myself, "I get paid to read the Bible!" I wanted to preach with accuracy, which is noble and a good Biblical pursuit. I was trying so hard to be 'right', my relationship with Jesus suffered, however. I'm not quite sure when it happened, but my Bible study and reading time shifted and became sermon research, and stopped being a daily time to simply be with Jesus.

I had made no intentional decisions. I still loved Him and wanted to serve Him. But the connection we once had was not quite what it used to be. I was into the details of preaching with accuracy and had somehow lost the simple wonder and mystery of who Jesus is.

My wife and I do a lot of Marriage coaching. We do premarital counseling, which is fun! We also work with married couples who need a tune-up or are even in crisis. Couples can reach an impasse and don't know how to navigate past it. They both state their cases and are resolute about their positions. Most of the time, it's easy to see why each party feels the way they do. They have good reasons. They have thought it through. They state their cases, and they are convinced they are right. They might very well be.

But the key to a life-giving fulfilling marriage is not about being right. It is about being reconciled with your spouse. It's about being connected deeply and soulfully to this other human being you have committed to serve until death do you part.

Marriage is a covenant. Not a contract. A contract is a relationship with your rights protected and your responsibilities minimized. A covenant is a relationship with your rights surrendered and all responsibilities assumed. It's about laying yourself down for the betterment of your partner. It's about knowing your partner will go to the mat for you, even to their own detriment if need be.

We tell couples who have reached an impasse they have a choice to make.

"You can be right or you can be reconciled, but you can't be both."

Let that settle for a minute.

Maybe you need to read that last sentence again.

Much like a marriage, our relationship with Jesus is an intimate one. It is one of spiritual and soulful connection. The symbolism of Jesus being the Bridegroom and we, His church, being the Bride is rich in scripture.

Much like any other relationship, we have a choice to make.

Will we be 'right' or will we be 'reconciled'

The Pharisees in this, and many other chapters, were so intent on being right about the Law they couldn't reconcile that Jesus was the Messiah. I am not suggesting, by any means, we stop studying the Bible. God's Word is alive and active. His Spirit will speak to us as we read the Scriptures. His presence will come and comfort us. So, please read your Bible and ask Him to speak to you through the pages.

But Father God wants an intimate relationship with us.

Does He want us to search the Scriptures and learn His attributes and grow in wisdom? Yes.

But more than that, He wants us to know Him deeply and personally. He wants us to let go of the self-imposed need to be right and fully embrace the mystery of who He is.

Without that kind of surrender, I'm not sure we can ever get to the intimacy our souls desire.

# My Prayer

*Father,*

*May my pursuit of the knowledge of You never replace my relationship with You. May the mystery of who You are override my need to be right.*

*Amen*

## What is the Spirit saying to You?

Your Reflection

_______________________________________________

_______________________________________________

_______________________________________________

_______________________________________________

Your Prayer

_______________________________________________

_______________________________________________

_______________________________________________

_______________________________________________

Today I will _______________________________________

# luke 21

# The Widow's Offering

1 As Jesus looked up, he saw the rich putting their gifts into the temple treasury. 2 He also saw a poor widow put in two very small copper coins. 3 "Truly I tell you," he said, "this poor widow has put in more than all the others. 4 All these people gave their gifts out of their wealth; but she out of her poverty put in all she had to live on."

# Luke 21 Reflection

## Jesus Looks Up

This is a heavy passage of scripture.

It's heavy to read about nation against nation. Kingdom against kingdom. It's tough to hear Jesus say some will be betrayed by parents, brothers and sisters, relatives and friends. Jesus even says it will be especially difficult for pregnant women and nursing mothers.

To be honest, the prophetic proclamation Jesus lays down here is dark.

Think about it. It was Jesus's last week of ministry leading up to the Crucifixion. His heart has to be heavy. His mind is processing the upcoming events He will have to go through.

The writer of Hebrews tells us Jesus 'endured the cross' for the joy set before Him. Yes, He did it willingly. He understood the assignment, but it's clear. He endured it. It was hard. Maybe that's why His tone is less than warm as He describes anguish, distress and people fainting from terror. When you read passages like this one, it can be easy to find oneself lost in how things are going to turn out. It's understandable to be more than a little afraid.

That's why I don't think it is a mistake immediately before Jesus starts talking about the Destruction of the Temple and the End Times, he takes time to notice the widow's offering. It almost feels like a random passing comment as the heaviness of the prophetic portion of the passage picks up.

Don't miss this. Right in the middle of the personal turmoil Jesus was experiencing, He saw the widow and her offering. He took time to notice her sacrifice and commend her for it.

His authority had just been questioned by the Pharisees in the previous chapter. He knew the church leaders were trying to find a way to kill Him. He is under constant scrutiny. He knows Judas will betray Him. It all has to be heartbreaking to Him. Now He has this dark prophetic message to deliver about the end times, which can't be an easy thing to have to say to people you love.

Don't let the weight of the moment pass you by. Jesus is dealing with some heavy personal and heartbreaking issues. It is in this moment Luke says,

"Jesus looked up and saw the widow."

That statement brings me a certain amount of peace when I feel overwhelmed by life and its troubles. It calms my heart when I feel overlooked by God because maybe He has too many world-shaking events to attend to to notice me and the fact I still need Him.

But I'm not overlooked.
> God is not too busy.
> > Jesus notices.
> > > He sees.

When my sons were younger and just getting into sports, they would ask me why they couldn't play a different position than the one they were playing. Because every little boy wants to be the star of the team. I was in leadership and understood the pressure of it. I was not about to go to the coach and tell him my son needs to play a different position. I was not going to be 'that' parent. I told my boys if you want an opportunity to play a different position, then work hard when the coach isn't watching. Because at some point, when you are working hard, the coach will see you. When the coach sees you working hard, he might give you an opportunity. If you get an opportunity, you will make the most out of it. Why? Because you were working hard when nobody was watching.

And ya know what? Those words proved to be true! Dad's advice worked out in their lives.

I am, by no means, likening Jesus to a crusty coach. But if a crusty coach takes notice of the efforts of a little boy working hard when nobody is watching, how much more does God see us when we are feeling overwhelmed and overlooked? How much more is our serving Him not in vain? How much more does He see us when we feel as though our efforts are making little to no difference?

Jesus looked up and saw the widow.

He sees me, too.

He sees you, too.

# My Prayer

*Father,*

*Help me to remember You are the God who sees. Nothing is out of your watch. Not one sheep ever went missing without Your notice. You are the God who leaves the 99 to rescue the 1. Help me to remember when I feel a little lost in the shuffle, You look up and see me.*

*Amen*

**What is the Spirit saying to You?**

Your Reflection

_______________________________________________

_______________________________________________

_______________________________________________

Your Prayer

_______________________________________________

_______________________________________________

_______________________________________________

Today I will _________________________________

# luke 22

## Judas Agrees to Betray Jesus

1 Now the Festival of Unleavened Bread, called the Passover, was approaching, 2 and the chief priests and the teachers of the law were looking for some way to get rid of Jesus, for they were afraid of the people. 3 Then Satan entered Judas, called Iscariot, one of the Twelve. 4 And Judas went to the chief priests and the officers of the temple guard and discussed with them how he might betray Jesus. 5 They were delighted and agreed to give him money. 6 He consented, and watched for an opportunity to hand Jesus over to them when no crowd was present.

## The Last Supper

7 Then came the day of Unleavened Bread on which the Passover lamb had to be sacrificed. 8 Jesus sent Peter and John, saying, "Go and make preparations for us to eat the Passover."

9 "Where do you want us to prepare for it?" they asked.

10 He replied, "As you enter the city, a man carrying a jar of water will meet you. Follow him to the house that he enters, 11 and say to the owner of the house, 'The Teacher asks: Where is the guest room, where I may eat the Passover with my disciples?' 12 He will show you a large room upstairs, all furnished. Make preparations there."

13 They left and found things just as Jesus had told them. So they prepared the Passover.

14 When the hour came, Jesus and his apostles reclined at the table. 15 And he said to them, "I have eagerly desired to eat this Passover with you before I suffer. 16 For I tell you, I will not eat it again until it finds fulfillment in the kingdom of God."

17 After taking the cup, he gave thanks and said, "Take this and divide it among you. 18 For I tell you I will not drink again from the fruit of the vine until the kingdom of God comes."

19 And he took bread, gave thanks and broke it, and gave it to them, saying, "This is my body given for you; do this in remembrance of me."

20 In the same way, after the supper he took the cup, saying, "This cup is the new covenant in my blood, which is poured out for you.[a] 21 But the hand of him who is going to betray me is with mine on the table. 22 The Son of Man will go as it has been decreed. But woe to that man who betrays him!" 23 They began to question among themselves which of them it might be who would do this.

24 A dispute also arose among them as to which of them was considered to be greatest. 25 Jesus said to them, "The kings of the Gentiles lord it over them; and those who exercise authority over them call themselves Benefactors. 26 But you are not to be like that. Instead, the greatest among you should be like the youngest, and the one who rules like the one who serves. 27 For who is greater, the one who is at the table or the one who serves? Is it not the one who is at the table? But I am among you as one who serves. 28 You are those who have stood by me in my trials. 29 And I confer on you a kingdom, just as my Father conferred one on me, 30 so that you may eat and drink at my table in my kingdom and sit on thrones, judging the twelve tribes of Israel.

31 "Simon, Simon, Satan has asked to sift all of you as wheat. 32 But I have prayed for you, Simon, that your faith may not fail. And when you have turned back, strengthen your brothers."

33 But he replied, "Lord, I am ready to go with you to prison and to death."

34 Jesus answered, "I tell you, Peter, before the rooster crows today, you will deny three times that you know me."

## God's Devil

What a heartbreaking chapter.

Judas agrees to betray Jesus. At the Last Supper, the disciples are once again discussing which one of them will be the greatest. Jesus prays in such anguish He sweats drops of blood. Jesus is arrested and beaten. Peter denies he even knows Jesus.

It doesn't feel like things are going well. It feels like it's over. It reads like the story is ending in a very bad way. Of course, we know that is not true! We know the ending of the story. We have the perspective to know these things have to happen for the redemption plan of God to be fulfilled. The disciples did not. This was real life for them. Jesus knew it was going to be hard for them.

There is a passage in the middle of the Last Supper. Jesus is serving the disciples and prophesying His crucifixion. He turns to Simon Peter and says, "Simon, Simon, Satan has asked to sift all of you as wheat."

Wait a minute …
    Did He just say Satan *asked*?
        Satan …
            *Asked … !?!?*

Yes. Satan had to ask permission to sift Peter and the disciples like wheat. Much in the same way, he needed permission to test Job. In Job's case, God actually gave him boundaries and told him what he could and could not do.

1 Peter 5:8 says "Be alert and of sober mind. Your enemy the devil prowls around like a roaring lion looking for someone to devour." NIV

The NKJV says it this way and I like it better.

"Be sober, be vigilant; because your adversary the devil walks about like a roaring lion, seeking whom he may devour."

It doesn't say he gets to devour whoever he wants. It says there are those he may devour. If there are those he may devour, then there are those he may not devour.

It's a wild thought, isn't it? Satan can't do whatever he wants.

He is not omnipresent.
> He is a single being, and he is not in all places at all times.

He is not omniscient.
> He is not all-knowing. He is clever and cunning. But he is not all-knowing.

He is not omnipotent
> He does not hold all power.

I wrote this earlier, but it bears repeating. The devil doesn't have free rein in our lives. It can be argued the only place he has in us are the places we give him. Jesus said in John 14:30 the enemy had nothing in Him. The enemy held no power. He had no foothold because Jesus was without sin. He had never given the enemy an inch.

But we do sin. Not always intentionally. We are broken, and we miss the Way of Jesus sometimes. We give the enemy 'place' without even knowing it. The cool part is once we identify areas we have surrendered to the enemy, we can reclaim those areas, repent and evict him from our lives.

At least that was my experience. That's what it felt like the day I had my 'coming to myself' moment. The day clarity came. The day the spirit of deception left. Pick whatever metaphor you like best. One moment I was spiritually asleep, and in the next moment, I was awake and able to begin making clear, rational decisions once again.

     LISTENING THROUGH LUKE

I'm not saying that my experience is the only way God does things. That type of thinking only leads down roads of disappointment and frustration as we try to deduce the Almighty God into patterns and formulas.

As if He can be deduced.
As if it is possible to find the end of the Infinite.
As if the created would outsmart the Creator.

No.  I'm not trying to find the edges and hem Him in. I'm trying to draw attention to the reality that even though it seemed like things were crashing in on all sides around Jesus, the disciples and God's plan of redemption, nothing could have been further from the truth. God's plan was still on full blast, and things were working out just as He had planned before the foundations of the universe.

That thought has helped me through some difficult times. Maybe you are experiencing some things that sure don't feel like God's plan is working.

I remember after I had come to my senses and we went through a few months of intense counseling, we had decided to move our family back to our home state. We literally spent our last dollar on a rental truck to haul our stuff back home. I knew two things. We were going to crash with my parents until we could find a place to live, and I had one month free in a storage unit for all of our belongings.

During the drive, I had a lot of quiet time to think and pray. My conversation with God went something like the following:

*"Are we finished? Me and You?"*
*"Have I made such a mess of things to where I can never be of use to the Kingdom again?"*
*"Did I just screw the whole plan up?"*
*"Are we done?"*

Those thoughts were running through my head when my phone rang. It was a lady whose kids had been in our ministry years before. She had sung on my worship team. We knew her and her family well, but had not spoken for some time. I was surprised to hear from her. We caught up with how things were going, when she said the following:

"I have been selected to be the leader of a weekend retreat. I believe the Holy Spirit wanted me to call you to see if you would be willing to serve as one of my spiritual directors."

Remember, I had just asked God if we were finished when this call came through.

I told her later about the timing of the call. I said I knew she picked up the phone and dialed it, but it sure did feel like Jesus on the line saying to me, "Bro ..... we are nowhere close to finished. We are only getting started."

I can honestly say the most rewarding and fulfilling ministry has come after what looked like the end. The world would call it over. To most, it would certainly have appeared that way. But God had a plan none of us would have imagined.

I want to encourage you. No pain is wasted. Ugly things can be made beautiful. Points of pain can become points of redemption and strength. I don't know what you may be dealing with nor do I know why. But I do know this. You don't have to be afraid. The devil is still the devil. But take heart. He's God's devil.

God is still God.

He is still Sovereign.

He still sees.

# My Prayer

*Father,*

*On days when it appears as though the enemy has finally had his way in my life, help me to remember even the enemy must submit to You. In times of turmoil or when things seem to be spinning out of control, help me to remember You are still on Your Throne, ruling and reigning. Help me to trust You are still God, You are still Sovereign, and You see me.*

*Amen*

## What is the Spirit saying to You?

Your Reflection

________________________________________

________________________________________

________________________________________

________________________________________

Your Prayer

________________________________________

________________________________________

________________________________________

________________________________________

Today I will _________________________________

# luke 23

1 Then the whole assembly rose and led him off to Pilate. 2 And they began to accuse him, saying, "We have found this man subverting our nation. He opposes payment of taxes to Caesar and claims to be Messiah, a king."

3 So Pilate asked Jesus, "Are you the king of the Jews?"
"You have said so," Jesus replied.

4 Then Pilate announced to the chief priests and the crowd, "I find no basis for a charge against this man."

5 But they insisted, "He stirs up the people all over Judea by his teaching. He started in Galilee and has come all the way here."

6 On hearing this, Pilate asked if the man was a Galilean. 7 When he learned that Jesus was under Herod's jurisdiction, he sent him to Herod, who was also in Jerusalem at that time.

8 When Herod saw Jesus, he was greatly pleased, because for a long time he had been wanting to see him. From what he had heard about him, he hoped to see him perform a sign of some sort. 9 He plied him with many questions, but Jesus gave him no answer. 10 The chief priests and the teachers of the law were standing there, vehemently accusing him. 11 Then Herod and his soldiers ridiculed and mocked him. Dressing him in an elegant robe, they sent him back to Pilate. 12 That day Herod and Pilate became friends—before this they had been enemies.

13 Pilate called together the chief priests, the rulers and the people, 14 and said to them, "You brought me this man as one who was inciting the people to rebellion. I have examined him in your presence and have found no basis for your charges against him. 15 Neither has Herod, for he sent him back to us; as you can see, he has done nothing to deserve death. 16 Therefore, I will punish him and then release him." [17] [a]

18 But the whole crowd shouted, "Away with this man! Release Barabbas to us!" 19 (Barabbas had been thrown into prison for an insurrection in the city, and for murder.)

20 Wanting to release Jesus, Pilate appealed to them again. 21 But they kept shouting, "Crucify him! Crucify him!"

22 For the third time he spoke to them: "Why? What crime has this man committed? I have found in him no grounds for the death penalty. Therefore I will have him punished and then release him."

23 But with loud shouts they insistently demanded that he be crucified, and their shouts prevailed. 24 So Pilate decided to grant their demand. 25 He released the man who had been thrown into prison for insurrection and murder, the one they asked for, and surrendered Jesus to their will.

## The Crucifixion of Jesus

26 As the soldiers led him away, they seized Simon from Cyrene, who was on his way in from the country, and put the cross on him and made him carry it behind Jesus. 27 A large number of people followed him, including women who mourned and wailed for him. 28 Jesus turned and said to them, "Daughters of Jerusalem, do not weep for me; weep for yourselves and for your children. 29 For the time will come when you will say, 'Blessed are the childless women, the wombs that never bore and the breasts that never nursed!' 30 Then

"'they will say to the mountains, "Fall on us!"
    and to the hills, "Cover us!"'[b]

31 For if people do these things when the tree is green, what will happen when it is dry?"

32 Two other men, both criminals, were also led out with him to be executed. 33 When they came to the place called the Skull, they crucified him there, along with the criminals—one on his right, the other on his left. 34 Jesus said, "Father, forgive them, for they do not know what they are doing."[c] And they divided up his clothes by casting lots.

35 The people stood watching, and the rulers even sneered at him. They said, "He saved others; let him save himself if he is God's Messiah, the Chosen One."

36 The soldiers also came up and mocked him. They offered him wine

vinegar 37 and said, "If you are the king of the Jews, save yourself."

38 There was a written notice above him, which read: this is the king of the Jews.

39 One of the criminals who hung there hurled insults at him: "Aren't you the Messiah? Save yourself and us!"

40 But the other criminal rebuked him. "Don't you fear God," he said, "since you are under the same sentence? 41 We are punished justly, for we are getting what our deeds deserve. But this man has done nothing wrong."

42 Then he said, "Jesus, remember me when you come into your kingdom.[d]"

43 Jesus answered him, "Truly I tell you, today you will be with me in paradise."

## The Death of Jesus

44 It was now about noon, and darkness came over the whole land until three in the afternoon, 45 for the sun stopped shining. And the curtain of the temple was torn in two. 46 Jesus called out with a loud voice, "Father, into your hands I commit my spirit."[e] When he had said this, he breathed his last.

47 The centurion, seeing what had happened, praised God and said, "Surely this was a righteous man." 48 When all the people who had gathered to witness this sight saw what took place, they beat their breasts and went away. 49 But all those who knew him, including the women who had followed him from Galilee, stood at a distance, watching these things.

# Luke 23 Reflection

## Salvation

The same people who welcomed Jesus into town, laying down palm branches and their cloaks, shouting, "HOSANNAH!!" only a week ago, are now shouting for His crucifixion. What happened? What shifted?

Hosannah is not a praise word. It is a desperate cry to be saved. It means, "Save us now!" These people were desperate. They had heard about the miracles. Maybe they had witnessed one or two. Some of them potentially were a part of the 5,000 who ate off of the two loaves and five fish. Perhaps an uncle was blind who now sees. They had bought in. Jesus had to be the Messiah!

Laying down their cloaks and palm branches was a risky thing to do. That was reserved for kings and lords. The Roman guards would randomly stop people in the street and ask, "Who is Lord?" If the reply was not, "Ceaser is Lord", there was likely harsh punishment. So, for the jews to be shouting "Honannah! Blessed is the King who comes in the Name of the Lord" was risky. Risky even unto death!

But they went there.
>They believed.
>>They trusted.

Jesus spent the whole week in Jerusalem, not acting like the people expected.

They expected Jesus to kick Roman butt and take Roman names. They expected him to turn over the Roman tables and tell the Romans to give to the Jews what was due the Jews!

Instead, Jesus turned over the Jewish tables and told the Jews to give Caesar what is due Caesar!

"This is not how you are supposed to be behaving, Jesus! Why are you siding with the enemy? Do you know how they have treated us? Do you know they demand we say 'Caesar is Lord? We have risked it all for you! We put our necks on the line for you! And this is how you respond?"

On the morning when Jesus is brought before Pilate, all the Jews gather to watch the showdown. This meeting looks very much like the meeting, centuries earlier, between Moses and Pharaoh. The imagery is not lost on the Jews. Moses whipped Pharaoh and all of Egypt with the plagues. Surely, Jesus has been waiting for this moment! What is He going to do?

Will He send the angel of death again and kill them all?

But Jesus did nothing. Jesus said nothing.

The Jewish crowd had to have been confused and crushed. They became angry and fell prey to the manipulation of the Jewish Council. The same people who shouted "Hosannah" in the streets one week earlier are now crying "Crucify Him!"

And Jesus willingly went to the cross.

And as He laid down His life.
> Even though they didn't know it …
> > Even though they couldn't see it …

He was giving them exactly what they cried out for.

Salvation. Absolutely stunning.

I have lived for a few years now. I have the perspective on my life to look back and see why things had to transpire the way they did. The hard times. The painful times. I can see much of it now, and I understand the 'why' and I can see that the hard and painful things led me to a better place.

But in the middle of those times when Jesus wasn't doing what I expected Him to do. When he disappointed me and I was hurt. When it made
more sense to me if He had not stayed silent and just answered my
prayers, I have to ask myself the question.

Would I have been …
	*Could* I have been part of the crowd shouting for his crucifixion?

I would like to believe that I would not have been swayed by the manipulation of the Jewish leaders. I would like to imagine I am above it
all. But I am not. If I'm being honest, there have been moments in my
life when I have quietly crucified Him in my heart. But unlike those Jews
2,000 years ago in Pilates courtyard, I didn't need the crowd to encourage me. I didn't need to be manipulated. I did it all by myself. I hung
Him there. I turned my back and left Him alone.

And still, regardless of my anger and my accusations towards Him, Jesus didn't give me what I was crying out for or thought I wanted. No. As
He did centuries ago, He gave me what He knew I needed.

Salvation.

# My Prayer

*Father,*

*Forgive me for the times when I have kicked and screamed rather than chose to trust You. Forgive me for all of the times that are to come when I will struggle to trust You.*

*Amen.*

**What is the Spirit saying to You?**

Your Reflection

_______________________________________________

_______________________________________________

_______________________________________________

_______________________________________________

Your Prayer

_______________________________________________

_______________________________________________

_______________________________________________

_______________________________________________

Today I will _______________________________________

# luke 24

## Jesus Has Risen

1 On the first day of the week, very early in the morning, the women took the spices they had prepared and went to the tomb. 2 They found the stone rolled away from the tomb, 3 but when they entered, they did not find the body of the Lord Jesus. 4 While they were wondering about this, suddenly two men in clothes that gleamed like lightning stood beside them. 5 In their fright the women bowed down with their faces to the ground, but the men said to them, "Why do you look for the living among the dead? 6 He is not here; he has risen! Remember how he told you, while he was still with you in Galilee: 7 'The Son of Man must be delivered over to the hands of sinners, be crucified and on the third day be raised again.' " 8 Then they remembered his words.

9 When they came back from the tomb, they told all these things to the Eleven and to all the others. 10 It was Mary Magdalene, Joanna, Mary the mother of James, and the others with them who told this to the apostles. 11 But they did not believe the women, because their words seemed to them like nonsense. 12 Peter, however, got up and ran to the tomb. Bending over, he saw the strips of linen lying by themselves, and he went away, wondering to himself what had happened.

## On the Road to Emmaus

13 Now that same day two of them were going to a village called Emmaus, about seven miles[a] from Jerusalem. 14 They were talking with each other about everything that had happened. 15 As they talked and discussed these things with each other, Jesus himself came up and walked along with them; 16 but they were kept from recognizing him.

17 He asked them, "What are you discussing together as you walk along?"

They stood still, their faces downcast. 18 One of them, named Cleopas, asked him, "Are you the only one visiting Jerusalem who does not know the things that have happened there in these days?"

19 "What things?" he asked.

"About Jesus of Nazareth," they replied. "He was a prophet, powerful in word and deed before God and all the people. 20 The chief priests and our rulers handed him over to be sentenced to death, and they crucified him; 21 but we had hoped that he was the one who was going to redeem Israel. And what is more, it is the third day since all this took place. 22 In addition, some of our women amazed us. They went to the tomb early this morning 23 but didn't find his body. They came and told us that they had seen a vision of angels, who said he was alive. 24 Then some of our companions went to the tomb and found it just as the women had said, but they did not see Jesus."

25 He said to them, "How foolish you are, and how slow to believe all that the prophets have spoken! 26 Did not the Messiah have to suffer these things and then enter his glory?" 27 And beginning with Moses and all the Prophets, he explained to them what was said in all the Scriptures concerning himself.

28 As they approached the village to which they were going, Jesus continued on as if he were going farther. 29 But they urged him strongly, "Stay with us, for it is nearly evening; the day is almost over." So he went in to stay with them.

30 When he was at the table with them, he took bread, gave thanks, broke it and began to give it to them. 31 Then their eyes were opened and they recognized him, and he disappeared from their sight. 32 They asked each other, "Were not our hearts burning within us while he talked with us on the road and opened the Scriptures to us?"

33 They got up and returned at once to Jerusalem. There they found the Eleven and those with them, assembled together 34 and saying, "It is true! The Lord has risen and has appeared to Simon." 35 Then the two told what had happened on the way, and how Jesus was recognized by them when he broke the bread.

## Jesus Appears to the Disciples

36 While they were still talking about this, Jesus himself stood among them and said to them, "Peace be with you."

37 They were startled and frightened, thinking they saw a ghost. 38 He said to them, "Why are you troubled, and why do doubts rise in your minds? 39 Look at my hands and my feet. It is I myself! Touch me and see; a ghost does not have flesh and bones, as you see I have."

40 When he had said this, he showed them his hands and feet. 41 And while they still did not believe it because of joy and amazement, he asked them, "Do you have anything here to eat?" 42 They gave him a piece of broiled fish, 43 and he took it and ate it in their presence.

44 He said to them, "This is what I told you while I was still with you: Everything must be fulfilled that is written about me in the Law of Moses, the Prophets and the Psalms."

45 Then he opened their minds so they could understand the Scriptures. 46 He told them, "This is what is written: The Messiah will suffer and rise from the dead on the third day, 47 and repentance for the forgiveness of sins will be preached in his name to all nations, beginning at Jerusalem. 48 You are witnesses of these things. 49 I am going to send you what my Father has promised; but stay in the city until you have been clothed with power from on high."

## The Ascension of Jesus

50 When he had led them out to the vicinity of Bethany, he lifted up his hands and blessed them. 51 While he was blessing them, he left them and was taken up into heaven. 52 Then they worshiped him and returned to Jerusalem with great joy. 53 And they stayed continually at the temple, praising God.

# Luke 24 Reflection

## Jesus is Kind

Amidst the drama of the last few days, the very ones who spent the last three years with Jesus have suddenly forgotten all He had said to them. He had poured into them. He had taught them. He connected Old Testament prophetic dots for them. He had revealed to them He was, indeed Messiah!

And now ……. they don't remember a thing.

To be fair, their whole world has been turned upside down. They had traveled with Jesus. They had seen Him do miracles. He had allowed them to be a part of those miracles! They watched as He brilliantly schooled the Pharisees. They watched the wind and waves obey Him.

They had to have been sure there was nothing that could stop Jesus. Now He's gone. Just like that. All of the hopes, dreams and future they were looking forward to are now gone.

Have you ever experienced a sudden and unexpected loss? It leaves you stunned and not quite sure what your next step is going to be. Imagine the confusion they were experiencing. All the waves of grief hitting them at once. Emotionally frozen over the loss of Jesus.

Also, think about the fear they must all have been in.

Can you even try to imagine the horror of watching the person for whom you left friends and family and have followed for three years be brutally crucified? Right there in the middle of town?

Knowing they may be coming for you next? They must have been unable to think, let alone process the moment.

Modern language would likely call it trauma.

They are all in hiding. The women have come back from the Garden to tell the people an angel has appeared to them and said Jesus is not in the tomb. He has risen!! They all say it's nonsense.

Peter runs to the tomb to see for himself. Even though Jesus had spoken of these events and tried to prepare the disciples for it, Luke tells us Peter saw the empty tomb but left wondering to himself what had happened.

Yet, Jesus shows up and walks them through it. He reveals himself in the most tender of ways. He isn't judging or scolding. He is giving them what they need in the moments when they can't see what they need for themselves.

The kindness of Jesus is beautiful.

The disciples in this story remind me of a 12-year-old boy whose mother tells him to clean his room. She holds his face in her hands. His cheeks are squished just a bit. She looks him directly in the eyes and gives him specific instructions on what to do when he gets there.

"Clean up your room.
 Pick up your clothes.
  Put them in the hamper.
   Make up your bed."

She even makes him repeat the instructions back to her. Which he does flawlessly. Through squeezed cheeks he repeats the instructions.

"Cwean up my woom.
 Pick up my cwothes.
  Put them in the hampuh..
   Make up my bed."

Then she gently spins him around and shoves him off to his room. Before he gets there, the things she just said and he repeated back to her, have somehow leaked out of his brain. He doesn't remember a word of it. Suddenly unsure of why he is in his room, the 12-year-old gives his shoulders a shrug and begins playing video games.

So it was with the disciples on Resurrection Morning.

Everything Jesus said has somehow leaked out of their brains and they are reeling. They are confused and afraid. How can the disciples not see what's happening? How can they not remember what Jesus said?

But when I take a moment and put myself in their position, I'm reminded there have been drama-filled moments in my life when I instantly freaked out and dove head first into the deep end of the pool of anxiety. Completely forgetting His promises of never leaving me and never forsaking me.

Just like the disciples, in the middle of my human weakness, Jesus comes and reminds me of everything He said and did. He reveals Himself in ways that were mysteriously hidden, and I was unable to see. Because of His comfort, I calm down. I lean into His promises. He will provide. He will sustain. My faith rises and the anxiety subsides.

I will be forever grateful for Jesus who comes to me in my moments of despair. Who comes when I can't see a way through. Who comes and simply reminds me of all of the things He said. He doesn't accuse. He doesn't shame me.

He holds my face in His hands and simply reminds me of what He said.

"Get off the video games.
  Clean up your room.
    Pick up your clothes.
      Put them in the hamper.
        Make up your bed"

# My Prayer



**What is the Spirit saying to You?**

Your Reflection

_______________________________________________

_______________________________________________

_______________________________________________

Your Prayer

_______________________________________________

_______________________________________________

_______________________________________________

Today I will _______________________________________

# acknowledgments

To Gwen - Thank you for the safe place you give me to open my heart. Thank you for crying along with me as I read the rough draft of each reflection to you. Without your support and belief in me, I'm not sure this project would have ever happened.

To the EPIC boys - Kyle, Marc, Blake, Clay, Devin, Felix, David, Hector, Lane, Paul, Peter and Harvey. I will never forget our year together. Thank you for the encouragement and support of my writing. You are truly my brothers.

# about the author

Mark Brague has served in ministry for over 20 years, sharing his passion for faith, worship, and helping others grow in their spiritual walk. His experience spans preaching, leading worship, and speaking to both men's and women's groups. Alongside his wife, Gwen, Mark leads couples coaching and marriage counseling, where together they host transformative weekend intensives focused on strengthening relationships. Their heart for people and commitment to authentic connection define their work. Mark and Gwen live out their ministry in the Metro Atlanta area.